## Author's Note

*Diminished Capacity* is a work of fiction, however, its content is based on a real-life criminal case of first-degree sexual assault.

Everything that happens in this novel during the jury trial, was carefully researched and is accurate to the best of the author's ability – but the names of every real person involved has been changed.

# PROGRAM

**ACT I**

Scene One:  The Prologue

Scene Two:  Attorney for the Defense

Scene Three:  The Briefcases

Scene Four:  The Evidence

Scene Five:  Lorna's Secret

Scene Six:  The Prison Meeting

**ACT II**

Scene One:  The Trial

Scene Two:  Witnesses for the Prosecution

Scene Three:  Hell Hath No Fury

Scene Four:  Witnesses for the Defense

Scene Five:  Genetics versus the Law

Scene Six:  The MidState Medical Center

Scene Seven:  A Drug Cocktail

**ACT III**

Scene One:  Closing Summations

Scene Two:  The Verdict

# DIMINISHED CAPACITY

## ACT I

### Scene One

## The Prologue

*Sunday, January 10, 2010.*

Pastor William McCord stands before the congregation at the Word of God Church in Cambridge, Minnesota, a small town forty-five miles north of Minneapolis-St. Paul. The religious service comes to a close.

"I wish you all a very blessed day. Now, go into our community, spreading God's word, and obeying His commandments. Amen and Amen."

The congregation responds.

"Thanks be to God."

The church empties, with the exception of one parishioner, Russell Swain. He waits until all the congregates have left, and walks to the front of the church where he is greeted by Pastor McCord and Charles Lynn, the director of Men's Sober Home, a residential program that assists male church members with alcohol- or drug-related addictions.

Swain had expressed a very strong desire to be a mentor in the volunteer program, and had met with Lynn the previous Friday evening to discuss an appointment. Upon completion of a very brief meeting, he was informed by Lynn that, because of his history of immature conduct, inappropriate comments, and a pattern of sudden irrational outbursts, he was not an acceptable candidate for such a position.

Enraged by the rejection, Swain responded characteristically by blurting out that he hadn't wanted the appointment in the first place, because it would only interfere with his real interests, including an array of personal sordid behaviors he listed matter-of-factly.

Greatly disturbed by what he just heard, Lynn quickly realized these admissions had to be witnessed by another person – preferably their pastor, William McCord.

Russell Swain is forty-three years old, six feet, four inches tall, and weighs well over three hundred pounds.

Frightened, but attempting to appear calm, Lynn asked if they could please meet with McCord after the following Sunday's service, to get a second opinion concerning Swain's acceptance as a mentor.

Swain angrily agreed.


The men are seated in the pastor's office after the Sunday service. McCord opens the meeting.

"Russell, after you and Chuck discussed your desire to be appointed a mentor, he informed you there was little possibility of that, and gave his reasons.  I agreed with him.  What was said after *that,* however, was so disturbing to him, he wouldn't repeat it to me, insisting it had to come from you."

Gone are Swain's haughtiness and the anger of that Friday's meeting.  Instead, he starts to sob heavily, strongly resembling a child, pleading with both men to reconsider.

McCord is embarrassed and puzzled by this behavior, but tries to assist.

"Open yourself up to God.  Confess your sins before Him, and empty your soul of all that is plaguing you.  I will then call upon the Holy Spirit for His decision."

Near to losing all control, Swain repeats Friday's statements.

McCord sits stunned at what he's hearing – a litany of sexual thoughts and behaviors.

Swain has now confessed to both men of the church his extensive, bizarre history of personal misconduct, which apparently continues to the present day.

He confesses that he has had sex with both women and men, with animals, has been involved in bondage and sadomasochistic thoughts and behaviors, and became excited while watching a DVD depicting a serial killer having sex with a woman before murdering her.

Russell Swain then admits to having sexual thoughts regarding society's most *intolerable* behavior.

Children.

Then, without giving a reason, Swain asks Lynn if he can now meet privately with McCord.  Lynn leaves the room and the two men are alone.

Swain proceeds to openly disclose for the first time, what had occurred that moved him from thoughts about children to a criminal behavior.

This tear-filled confession will drastically alter the remainder of his life.

In the absence of any concern for the personal consequences, or perhaps thinking McCord would not divulge his confession, he reveals to his pastor that he sexually assaulted an underage female on January 2, 2010 – a week and a half prior to this meeting.

The victim is his twelve-year old daughter.

Shortly after his confession, Lynn returns to the room and tells Swain he was to give McCord and his family a ride home, and must leave soon.  The meeting ends.

During the ride home, the pastor appears visibly shaken. Seeing his wife and their two children are in the back seat, he does not tell Lynn what Swain said when the two of them were alone.  However, without looking at Lynn, he says:

"Please pray for me … and for what I must do."

The next morning, Pastor McCord telephones the Isanti County Sheriff's Office, and informs a deputy of Swain's admission he had sex with his minor daughter.

Russell Howard Swain is arrested on the highway that late afternoon, as he drives home to Cambridge from the St. Paul junior high school where he teaches mathematics.

## Scene Two

# Attorney for the Defense

*Two years later. Nine a.m., Wednesday, February 15, 2012.*

Jeremiah Bedloe enters his law office on the fourth floor of the old Hoeschler Building in downtown La Crosse, Wisconsin.

His secretary, Lorna Dunn, greets him.

"Good morning, JB."

"Yeah."

"How're you feeling this beautiful day?"

Bedloe removes his rabbit fur-lined leather gloves, long brown woolen overcoat and plaid scarf, and throws it all on a chair in the client's waiting area. As he takes off his black stocking cap, he looks out the office window at the Arctic freeze and crisply responds.

"You know, whether it be rain or shine, sleet or snow, that same *damn* question is asked every time your spies tell you I went out for a few drinks after work. If you must inquire, I feel briskly energetic this beautiful morn', despite my faithful secretary being a terribly *flagitious* female."

Bedloe throws the cap onto the pile of clothes. Lorna replies:

"Well, that may be so, if I knew the meaning of that word."

Lorna gets up from her desk and walks to the pile of outer garments, playfully shaking her head with a judgmental facial expression. She scoops them up, and keeps on with the exchanges while going to a small clothes closet to hang them up, an office practice she's learned to tolerate.

"The minute you walk through the door, I know you stayed out late by the way you look. What's that called, 'the morning after the night before?' I just can't help but wonder why a man such as you keeps on trying to kill himself with that stupid liquid sin – especially someone your age."

"Oh, spare me your angelical decrees, will you please. And, if you don't know what the hell the meaning of a simple word like *flagitious* is, then look it up in your damn … Funk and Wagnalls."

Lorna slowly and deliberately places fists firmly on her hips and with head cocked to one side, ignores the curse words. She smiles.

"You're showing your age, JB. That TV show, *Laugh-In*, was a little before my time, you know. But, I do remember it from re-runs, once I got old enough to watch them."

"All right, all right, get me a cup of coffee and cut the Hawkeye sarcasm crap. I'm not in the mood. What do I have today?"

Lorna goes to pour the coffee, and then returns carrying the cup by the handle in one hand, the appointment book in the other.

"You're to be in La Crosse County Court at ten fifteen, the Marian Yeske case. That'll probably go to pret'-near noon. Then at, let's see, two fifteen this afternoon" – she says with more tongue-in-cheek humor – "just about the time you're getting back from your lunch break … here," and hands him the cup.

"You're to have an initial appointment with a Mr. Michael Swain."

He looks at her with a reciprocal grin, wrapping his hand around the cup without thinking.

"Ouch. Jesus Christ! Why didn't you tell me it was so fricking hot?"

He knew better than to hit her with the "F-bomb".

"That'll be for all the cussing, and for taking the Lord's name in vain. You're going straight to hell for that one."

"Tell me something I don't already know. I do know one thing, I sure as *hell* won't see you there. What's this Swain want to talk about?"

"His son's in a Minnesota prison, and he wants you to get him released."

"A Minnesota prison? Fat chance."

*Loma Dunn has been attorney Jeremiah Bedloe's personal secretary and receptionist since 1988, starting just after completing the legal secretary program at Western Wisconsin*

*Technical College in La Crosse. She was raised on a farm near Lansing, Iowa, thirty miles south of La Crosse on the other side of the Mississippi River. Lorna has the Midwestern work ethic of a pioneer woman leading a team of horses hitched to a plow, and she manages the office in the same manner. She has never missed a day of work in her life, routinely skipping lunch to do what needs to be done.*

*In her mid-forties, she's a somewhat portly woman now, with an ultra-conservative short and tightly-curled hair-do. Her law office attire is always loose fitting one-piece dresses hemmed well below the knee, and never wears make-up. She's been married to the same man, Victor, for twenty years. He works at Lansing Coop Feed and Seed. They have one daughter in high school and all are very active members of Our Savior's Lutheran Church in Lansing.*

*Their old but immaculate two-story wooden frame house sits just on the edge of the village and she commutes every day to work. They enjoy small town living and cannot imagine moving into the hustle-bustle of "city life" in La Crosse.*

*Attorney Jeremiah Bedloe moved to La Crosse, Wisconsin from Chicago's northwest side in 1978, and continues to maintain his thick Windy City accent. He grew weary of the metropolis's pace, and has since been practicing criminal law in this far smaller and laid-back picturesque city of fifty thousand people on the banks of the Mississippi River. Twice divorced with three grown children, he rents a large studio apartment in what was an ornate late nineteenth-century mansion on Cass Street that was built by an early lumber magnate and his family.*

*Known for years as a man who drinks too often and too much, his reputation is nevertheless that of a successful professional who meets his daily responsibilities. He is commonly thought of in southwest Wisconsin and southeast Minnesota – he is licensed to practice law in both states – as an attorney with expansive legal knowledge with a ferocious yet controlled temper. His brushes with censure and disbarment are the stuff of area legend, yet he continues to maintain a casual attitude about testing the limits of legal conduct.*

*Bedloe, though in his late sixties, has the stature of and facial resemblance to Clarence Darrow, and also embraces Darrow's wit and agnosticism, along with a professional worship of his judicial folk hero. When in a serious trial debate, Bedloe's eyes become intimidating to the most seasoned lawyers or witnesses for the prosecution. His voice is vibrant and deep, and grand volume that easily fills the courtroom without needing artificial sound amplification.*

*His selection of professional attire is casual, even a little sloppy, and usually consists of old tan cotton trousers, a corduroy sport coat with suede patches on the elbows, and suede loafers. Photographs of mid-twentieth century professors and lawyers often pictured them in similar attire, so Bedloe proudly emulates them. He stubbornly believes these great intellectuals measured themselves by the content of their craniums, not by what covered their bodies.*

*His apartment is as unkempt as his salt-and-pepper hair. The oversized living area has a sofa bed with one end table, a kitchen table and two chairs, and a desk with a swivel chair. The rest is wall-to-wall shelves of books directly or indirectly* concerned with the practice of law. He has no television set and doesn't know the slightest thing about computers or other contemporary gadgets, including a cell-phone. He refuses to own any of it, because he feels they're "a waste of the human experience," which may also be an indication he refuses to acknowledge that time may very well be passing him by.

Though an admitted throwback, he proudly drives his cherry 2008 red Corvette with an uncharacteristically impeccable tan vinyl top and leather interior. And, as might be expected, his license plate reads "JB 1."

Life is swiftly reaching its last act for the man, and a once lucrative law practice saturated with high profile cases, has recently been scaled back due to repetitive boredom. Financially successful, he now accepts DUI and spousal battery cases just to have enough to pay the bills and live on, and to keep semi-active in a profession he continues to love.

Anyone who has ever met Bedloe inside or outside of the courtroom knows that God truly intended him to be a lawyer. And, all of them will attest to the fact that this man has an unabashed toughness and honesty that serves him well.

Despite the inner contentment he's earned knowing he has been highly successful in his legal career, there is still something missing in his professional life, a hole yet to be filled. In the quiet of the evenings, he sits alone on his sofa among the clutter of books and papers, reading and clutching an old friend wrapped in glass. He occasionally stares at the wall behind his desk, covered with framed accolades and awards.

*He is well aware of what the vacancy in his life consists of, but realizes that in this part of the country, it will not likely come to pass – the ultimate courtroom drama, a challenge worthy of Darrow – a major trial he can deeply sink his teeth into, wildly gnawing and consuming until his belly is full, then exiting this world with a satisfyingly loud belch.*

*Jeremiah Bedloe, attorney-at-law, may soon be provided with that trial.*

## Scene Three

# The Briefcases


*The northern Midwestern winter climate is referred to by many as the frozen tundra, and today it is below zero with a wind chill factor in the sub teens. With at least a foot of hard snow covering the ground, it's certainly living up to its reputation. Jeremiah Bedloe has the prized Corvette stashed away, hibernating in a local heated garage, and walks the seven blocks to and from his office almost every working day. When he has an appointment or socializes somewhere that is not within walking distance this time of year, he calls a cab. When there's a need to travel out of town, he rents a car from a local dealership. He's lived in this climate all his life, and wouldn't live anywhere else, but at times he seriously considers cuddling up next to his sports car and sleeping until spring.*


*It is 2:10 p.m. that afternoon.*


"How was lunch, JB?"

"Good. Yours?"

"Didn't go."

"Why don't you go now? I can hold down the fort 'til you get back."

"Nah, I should shed a few pounds. Besides, there's too much to do."

"You're the boss, my dear, therefore, you always know best."

Bedloe takes off the outer garments and throws them back onto the same chair. He sees an older guy with long silver and blondish hair in a pony-tail sitting in the waiting area. Walking to his office, he glances at him again and notes the tan face and hands sticking out from the man's winter coat.

A last glance also notes two large briefcases on the floor alongside him.

He enters his office and sits down in the overstuffed leather chair behind his desk. After Lorna hangs up her boss' coat and puts away his hat, scarf and gloves, she comes in with the man carrying the briefcases.

"JB, this is Mr. Michael Swain. Mr. Swain, Mr. Jeremiah Bedloe."

Bedloe stands up and reaches across the desk with his hand extended. Lorna turns and walks back to her desk and leaves the attorney's door open – which lets her see and hear everything, a practice Bedloe insists on so that he has a witness to what transpires.

Michael Swain puts one of the briefcases down and shakes the attorney's hand.

"Good afternoon, Mr. Swain. Sit down."

"Thank you."

Swain goes to stand in front of one of the two client chairs facing Bedloe's desk, while the attorney sits and leans back, joining his hands across his stomach. Swain takes off his long heavily insulated coat, probably recently purchased, puts it on another chair next to him, and sits down. He is wearing Levi jeans and a colorful short-sleeved shirt filled with palm trees and tropical flowers.

Bedloe grins and puts the hands behind his head with fingers still intertwined. Swain aggressively rubs his hands together, then blows on them in a futile attempt to get warm.


*Michael Swain is about the same height as Bedloe, but other than that, there is no physical resemblance. He looks much younger looking than Bedloe, despite being close to the same age. And he still has an athletic build that suggests an ongoing effort to defy the aging process.*

*Swain is modest and conservative, yet there's an "edge" to him that tells people he has a tough side if pushed too far.*


Bedloe says, "I trust you haven't been waiting too long."

"Walked in just before you," Swain replies. "Man, I'd forgotten how cold it can get up here!"

"I'd say you're not used to this weather."

"I just got in from south Florida, leaving a sunny seventy-eighty degrees behind me."

"It must be damn important that you be here, leaving that behind."

"It is very important."

"Before we start discussing your son, tell me a little bit about yourself."

"Well, I moved to La Crosse in '64, went to the university, graduated with a bachelor's degree in '68, a master's degree in '72. Then I went to work for W.W.T.C. shortly after that – until I retired in 1998."

Bedloe smiles. "A long time. So, you're from La Crosse. Incidentally, it's now called W.T.C., 'Western Technical College.' They shed the 'W' for Wisconsin. I go over there and have lunch in the cafeteria every so often, and have been for a long while."

"Yes, sir. I know. I recall seeing you there years ago. I also remember some of what I heard about you, you know, a grapevine kind of thing. Don't get me wrong, most of it was complimentary. As a matter of fact, that's why I'm here."

"Mr. Swain, it's irrelevant to me what you heard.

"Where in south Florida do you live?"

"Palm City. It's between Vero Beach and West Palm, just outside of Stuart – right off I-95."

"Nice. I envy you, especially this time of year. Well, maybe not.

"Oh, by the way, what did you do for the college?"

"I was a counselor in the Department of Counseling and Testing."

"Interesting, considering the present circumstances with your son. Are you married?"

Swain ignores the little dig. "No, sir. My wife and I were divorced in '89. I've been single ever since."

"You have one son in a Minnesota prison. Anymore kids?"

"A younger son who lives in Appleton. He's a deputy sheriff there."

Bedloe sits up straight, hands still joined, but now resting on his desktop.

"Well, one out of two isn't a bad average. Lorna, my secretary, tells me the son in prison wants legal assistance in trying to get released. How long's he in for?"

Swain glares at the attorney, and answers.

"Fifteen years."

The look doesn't faze Bedloe. "What'd he do?"

Swain pauses and looks down, suddenly embarrassed.

"He sexually assaulted a girl. First degree."

Bedloe's demeanor changes from introductory conversation to deadpan serious. He also looks down and slowly shakes his head back and forth.

"First degree, huh?  Knowing Minnesota, he's lucky that's all he got."  He looks up.  "What's the girl's age?"

"She was twelve when it happened.  It was the start of 2010, just after New Year's.  So, she'll, uh, be fourteen on July twenty-third."

"Twelve?  Well, that explains the first degree.  How old is your son?"

"Forty-five now."

"You know the girl's birthday."

Swain nods.

"How do you know that?"

Swain again shakes his head slowly from side to side, still looking to the floor.

"She's his daughter.  My granddaughter."

He puts both hands over his face and starts to nervously rub his forehead with the fingertips.  The attorney looks out the office window, then asks another question.

"Does he have any other kids?"

"No, sir."

There is a very awkward silence and Bedloe glances at Lorna, who stares at her employer with an appalled look on her deeply reddened face like none he had ever seen on his secretary before this day.  Matching red watery eyes glare at him, her body seems to be shaking, clearly indicating she's intensely angry. Furious. He returns to Swain.

"Look, I'm a pretty straightforward guy, even for a lawyer, and I don't B.S. anyone. Let me ask you a question. How in the *hell* do you expect me, or any attorney for that matter, to get your son out of prison after what he did? You're telling me he did it."

Swain looks up and nods.

"Yes, sir. He did it, he surely did it. As a matter-of-fact, he confessed to it right away. He wasn't found guilty by a jury, but by a judge at a sentencing hearing."

"Did he confess before or after consulting with a defense attorney?"

"That's one of the reasons I'm here. You see ..."

Bedloe decides to change the subject because he's still gathering preliminary information, and senses Swain wants to get into the crux of the case. It's too soon.

"Is he married to the girl's mother?"

"No, sir. They're divorced. But he remarried a couple years ago. She has two children."

"How old are they?"

"The boy is thirteen now, I think. The girl is eleven, perhaps twelve."

Bedloe again looks at Lorna. She's staring down at her desk with a blank, bewildered expression. After all these years, he can almost read her mind. She's wondering if his son did anything to those kids. He looks back at Swain.

"Was this his second marriage, third?"

"Second."

"Where do they live?"

"Cambridge, Minnesota, north of the Cities. His wife has a house there."

"So then, you must know I'm licensed in Minnesota."

Swain nods. "Yes, sir."

Bedloe smiles. "You don't have to call me, 'sir.' 'Jeremiah' is fine, 'Jerry' isn't. And I'll call you 'Michael' instead of 'Mike.' A deal?"

Swain shrugs his shoulders. "Whatever."

"Did she divorce him after he was arrested?"

"No. She's still sticking by him, up until now anyway. So are the kids."

"They are? Why?" Clearly questioning how anyone could possibly do that.

"Because, she says, that's just not the Russell they know."

"That's his name, Russell Swain?"

"Yes."

"How about you?  Is that the Russell Swain *you* know?  Is that your son?"

"No.  I've known for some time, that he started to change before this happened, especially in 2009.  He was starting to show signs, symptoms of mental disorders.  Serious ones.  His wife noticed it as well.

"He was seeing a lot of doctors.  As a matter-of-fact, after learning what I know now, my granddaughter is probably lucky to be alive today."

"If you believe that, then maybe he *is* where he should be.  But are you implying these mental disorders made him do what he did to his daughter?"

"Mr. Bedloe – Jeremiah – when I heard what he did to her, I also believed he is where he ought to be, just like everybody else."

Swain leans forward in his chair.

"But the day he was sent to prison, something happened to me.  I don't know if you believe in God, but I do.  I think I'm a religious man, but not a fanatic or anything.  I worship silently, and don't parade it around for everyone to see and hear.  Something came over me, something led me to look for answers."

"Answers?  Answers to what?"

"I thought to myself, why did Russell do this? It doesn't make any sense.  The man has a master's degree and was a middle-school math teacher in St. Paul.  He and his wife were making well over a hundred thousand bucks a year and living in a beautiful home in the country. His step-kids love him, and his daughter gets along with all of them. Jeremiah, believe me, he loves his daughter and she loves him. It's such a terrible tragedy."

"Michael, you're obviously an intelligent man, and given what you did at the college, certainly you must be aware that pedophiles come from all walks of life."

Swain becomes angry and is clearly very offended by the word "pedophile." He shoots back at Bedloe.

"Yes, I do know *that!* But I'll believe it *only* after everything is looked into. There are just *too* many unanswered questions."

"Had he been in trouble with the law before? Sex with a minor? Forcible sex of any kind? Anything?"

Swain shakes his head. "No. Just this one incident."

"So, as far as you know, there've been no other victims?"

"Well, according to the prosecutor at the court sentencing hearing there were. She got her information from the Alpha Human Services' report, a Twin Cities' agency that did the screening interview to determine if Russ would be accepted into their residential sex offender treatment program. But it was all twisted around, distorted, to sound like there *were* other victims."

Bedloe puts his hands over his ears and shakes his head, clearly confused.

"Wait, wait, wait. You're going from a happy home life to mental disorders. From loving parent to sex offender. From a master's degree to prison and treatment centers, and I don't know what else is yet to come."

Swain attempts to clarify. He knows the secretary is listening, so he leans even farther forward, and whispers to Bedloe.

"Russ was into porn for some time, probably for years. This was all brought out in the various reports, and at the sentencing hearing. The prosecutor felt strongly that there was a very definite connection between the three; the porn, the disorders, and the assault. Okay?"

The defense attorney remains confused, but says, "Okay."

Swain continues with the whisper.

"The prosecutor tried to show that my son had everything from an anti-social personality disorder to a narcissistic personality disorder, from being an incestuous pedophile to being a voyeur and an exhibitionist. She successfully convinced the judge that these patterns of behavior actually existed, but they *don't!* I now feel *strongly* that there were other *more* important reasons the court didn't hear about, or care about."

In keeping with his often sarcastic mannerisms, Bedloe leans forward in *his* chair, close to Swain's face, and whispers back:

"What reasons?"

Picking up on Bedloe's jocular mockery, Swain lightly taps both briefcases and imitates the attorney's whisper:

"It's all in here."

Bedloe grins widely, as he picks up on Swain's compatible personality, so he continues the "game."

"What's in there?"

Swain slumps back, pauses for a moment, takes a deep breath, and then continues in normal voice.

"'I had a lap top computer a couple years back but dropped it and broke the screen, so it was a goner.  It was only used for e-mails and an occasional website search, so instead I went to the library to use theirs a couple of times a week.  When Russ was sent to prison, I started going more and more, but now to look things up on the internet, like sexual disorders, sex crimes, psychological factors and psychiatric prison records.  The hits that came up sent me to other sites and different possible explanations and answers to my questions."

He sits up straight, then continues.

"I wore a path between the computer and the printer, making copies of everything.  Finally, I went and bought one of my own, took it home and spent hundreds of hours reading, printing, and typing about everything I could find."

Bedloe looks at the briefcases and nods towards them.

"I've got a feeling *that's* what's in those?"

Swain nods, "Yes, that and much, much more."

He excitingly reaches down to one of the briefcases and unlatches it.

"Here, can I show you something? It's a paper I wrote on my son's case, and the possible reasons why he did what he did."

Swain produces a thick, professional-looking spiral bound treatise and tries to hand it to Bedloe, who looks at it and immediately puts his hands up in a "halt" gesture.

"Before this goes any further, let me see if I'm getting it so far. You know your son is guilty, right? He confessed. But now you believe the information in those briefcases will somehow explain why he sexually assaulted his daughter. And I've got a hunch this information is for the purpose of showing he is not responsible for committing the crime. That some mental impairment is responsible? Is that what this is all about? Is that what I'm hearing?"

Bedloe sits back with elbows on the chair's armrests, the fingertips of his hands lightly touching.

"And, this one's the 'kicker' – the reason you're here to see me, is to get him out of prison because he doesn't belong there, because of what you think you've found."

Bedloe pauses momentarily and stares at this father. Swain is about to respond, but Bedloe quickly waves his hand back and forth to indicate he has something more to add.

"What you seem to be getting at, is that you believe your son had no control over what he did. Are we talking about an after-the-fact *insanity* plea here? If it is, then let me save you a bundle of legal fees.  Minnesota doesn't recognize *diminished capacity.*"

"Diminished capacity?"

"I'll get into that later if necessary.  For right now, please tell me if 'insanity' is, or is not, what this is all about."

Swain pauses to think.

"I don't know.  It could be ... no, *no!*  It's *not* about that.  Look, I've lost count of how many Minnesota people I've sent this to," pointing to his ninety-page paper.

"Not one person has responded, or perhaps even taken the time to read any of it – the governor, attorney general, a whole bunch of state politicians, Mayo, university hospitals, the A.C.L.U., the Innocence Project, the media, and on and on and on.  Probably because of what Russ did, they just don't give a shit about him because of that!"

He reflexively turns and looks at Lorna.  "Excuse me, ma'am."  Noting the woman's extremely disturbed facial expression, Swain's gaze nevertheless returns to Bedloe.

"It could be it's because I'm his father, so the first thing they're going to think is that I'm just trying to get him off.  I guess I'd think that too.  But I've got an 'ace up my sleeve' when it comes to that."

His eyes suddenly flare with icy rage, his lips tighten.

"What he did, he did to my granddaughter.  My *granddaughter!*  That more than angers me, it *disgusts* me.

32

"God only knows what she must've been going through since then. This whole thing is filled with so much sorrow."

While listening, Bedloe again looks toward Lorna's desk, but this time she's nowhere in sight. Swain leans back and stares at the ceiling, adding with obvious emotional and mental fatigue:

"You know, at times I'm close to accepting what everyone else believes. But to my way of thinking, as I sit here today, he either knew what he was doing and could've controlled himself, and therefore he would no longer be my son, or ..."

Swain aggressively moves closer and stares into Bedloe's eyes, tapping his index finger hard and loud on the attorney's desk to emphasize key words.

"- or he *didn't* know what he was doing, and *couldn't* control himself. That's the bottom line, *that's* why I'm here. Something happened to him, and I now know what that 'something' was!"

Bedloe gets up and walks to the office window. He turns to face Swain in pure candor.

"Michael, I don't know you or your son. What I do know is that during the preliminaries preceding his sentencing hearing, the court gave him the opportunity to have a trial by jury. Instead, he pleaded guilty, thereby relinquishing that right. The court determined your son was of sound mind when he entered the guilty plea. Even without looking at the preliminary report, I can assure you, if there was anything he said or did that showed him to be incapable of understanding his plea, the court would not have accepted it.  Or, your son's attorney wouldn't have entered it."

Swain replies.  "His lawyer was worthless, and the record clearly showed he wasn't even trying.  The hearing was a sham!  He was even joking with the prosecutor while my son was led out after being sentenced to prison. Jeremiah, I ask you to *please* look at this!"

He again offers the thick report to Bedloe, who glances at his watch, then impatiently walks toward Swain and takes it with a deep, prolonged sigh.  He sits back down and starts to scan the pages in silence, doing so for a significant length of time.  Swain realizes a change in the attorney's facial expression and concentration, and that he may finally be getting someone's attention.

Bedloe seems so absorbed in what he's reading, Swain strategically starts to add more.  He goes again into the briefcase and gives Bedloe the MidState Medical Center's report on his son for the year 2009, just prior to the sexual assault.  He then withdraws his son's medical records and reports from various other Minnesota and Wisconsin clinics dating back to the early 1990s, as well as a complete psychosexual evaluation from a forensic psychologist and a psychological evaluation report from a clinical psychologist, both done while Russell Swain was in the Isanti County Jail.

After twenty minutes of scanning the papers, it is becoming abundantly clear to Bedloe that this father and grandfather has done a ton of homework.  It is equally evident he may even know what he's talking about.

Jeremiah Bedloe, a seasoned "trial-hardened" defense attorney, stares at what has been extracted from Swain's briefcase, thinking all the while that he has never heard of any parent ever doing what this man has done for his child. *Never.* And Swain has only opened up *one* of the two briefcases. He asks a question.

"How did you come by all these reports and documents?"

"I sent for them. I have power-of-attorney over matters concerning my son."

Bedloe obviously doesn't have time to read everything, however, he looks closely at one document – the ten-page report from the MidState Medical Center, the contents of which are lit up with Swain's yellow highlighter. He quickly notes the list of psychiatrists and psychologists, physical and psychological disorders, and especially the medications prescribed to Swain's son. He asks another question.

"May I keep these for a couple days?"

"Yes, certainly. I'm grateful that you'll take the time. I'll leave it all for you to look over. Thank you."

Michael Swain again leans over the armrest on his chair and returns a few papers still in his hand to the briefcase, then zippers it shut. He stands. As he does, Bedloe gets up from his chair, puts the papers already in his possession on the desk, and walks to the office door.

"Stick around for a few minutes. I need to ask you a couple more questions."

As he goes, he looks out at Lorna, who is now standing and staring at him with cold, insistent eyes.

She slowly shakes her head back and forth, while simultaneously nonverbally forming the word "no" on her lips.

He reaches for the door and closes it.

## Scene Four

# The Evidence

*The same day, around eight p.m.*

There is a knock on Jeremiah Bedloe's apartment door.

"Mr. Bedloe, its Thompson."

He is the manager of Bedloe's apartment building.

"Just a minute, Thompson."

He puts his brandy and ice on the end table and walks to the door.

"What can I do for you this frozen February night, my man?"

"Well, I'm fearin' it's gonna get colder.  The furnace ain't workin' too good.   You might be a little chilly tonight.  I'm goin' around tellin' everyone, thought ya might wanna know.  I got the guy comin' to look it over, hopefully we'll get'er goin' full force before sun up.  'Fraid ya may have'ta bundle up 'til then.  Sorry, Mr. Bedloe.  Good night, sir."

Bedloe puts a hand on Thompson's shoulder, and with a slight slurring of his words, he responds:

"Goodnight, my compadre.  The knowledge you have graciously bestowed upon me, will eliminate any personal hesitation concerning the partaking of consumable antifreeze, the purpose of which will be to warm my body and my soul 'til comfort doth once more engulf me."

Bedloe bows deeply, stumbling slightly. Thompson smiles and leaves, shaking his head, barely understanding a word of what was just said, and not really trying to all that hard.

The attorney closes the door and walks back to the sofa to sit. He had taken home the briefcases left for him to look over and they are just out of reach near the desk. He stares at them, trying to determine the wisdom of opening and examining something that should perhaps remain closed. While continuing to sip his brandy, sobering thoughts of his own daughter come to him. Yet, the contents of the papers read that afternoon dominate his mind.

Russell Swain's daughter could easily be forgotten, and replaced with the facts as to why this crime was committed – if they can be found. Laughing with mild intoxicated confidence, he looks again at the briefcases.

"Find the facts, the evidence? Hell, his father, Michael, beat me to it."

Secure in the privacy of his apartment, Bedloe starts to dramatically speak aloud in generalities to a non-existent jury, defending the yet to be determined client.

"How dare we provide facts, therefore relinquishing the *victim's* rights to justice. However, is justice served when *another* victim remains imprisoned due to prejudice towards a crime society deems intolerable?  Evil is inherent in man, as Greek mythology would have us believe.  I've seen my fill."  He goes on.

"The world *is* evil.  Any fool knows that, except those with heads deeply submerged in anything that provides escape to the world of ignorance."

The defense lawyer takes a large gulp that leaves the glass empty.  He puts it down hard on the end table, then aggressively lifts himself from the sofa and continues.

"Is evil the result of a single act or the repetition of that act?  Was this man the victim along with his daughter, her by a mortal man, him by worldly carelessness and biased stupidity?  Contemporary thought would have us believe that *all* men *are* evil, therefore easily portrayed as legally guilty the moment the crime is exposed.  Innocence be damned.

"*Zero tolerance* without regard to logic or reason!"

Bedloe picks up his glass and goes to the small kitchen, refills it with brandy and fresh ice while his soliloquy continues.  He then turns abruptly with drink in hand, a portion of which spills to the floor.  His other hand points an index finger to the mythological heavens, deeply immersed in legal argument.

When his statement is complete, the drink is tenderly placed on the end table and the late autumn-aged man falls gently onto the sofa, laughing in self-depreciation.  Engulfed in his own folly, he slumps spread-eagled onto the sofa, stating in exaggeratedly thick drunken speech while doing so:

"I have no goddamned *fucking* idea what the hell I'm talking about."


The walk to the office the next morning is a welcome wake up slap in the face. Bedloe spent the night slumped there on the sofa, not so much passed out, but rather in deep, prolonged thought until sleep inevitably consumed him.

The glass remains on the end table, still completely filled with a watery, clear brown solution.

When he arrives, Lorna is already at the file cabinet and does not acknowledge him, nor says a word. He again throws the wintery outer garments onto the same chair and goes into his office. Within five minutes, she stands at the door.

"Well?"

"Well what, Lorna? Well what?"

"You know what."

"I don't know yet. I haven't made up my mind. There's still a lot to think about and cover."

Bedloe walks to get his own coffee and his secretary follows him. He pours the coffee, then silently returns to his office. Lorna's right behind, which is clearly irritating him, so she returns to her desk and sits down. He turns around at the office door and speaks empathetically.

"Lorna, I think I know how you feel. I guess if ..."

She uncharacteristically raises her voice to her employer.

*"You have no idea how I feel!"*

Her eyes stare crazily at Bedloe, then suddenly she is subdued.

"No idea."

There's a momentary silence.

"You're right. You're absolutely right. I don't have any idea."

Bedloe is sincere and his voice is soft. He is shocked at his secretary's sudden angry reaction, reading into what might be the reason.

"Could be it's a 'woman thing?' I'm a man, not a woman. I've never been a woman."

Lorna looks to the ceiling and rolls her eyes in frustration over her boss' glib comments. Bedloe realizes his mistake.

"Okay, okay. Go ahead, tell me how you feel. I want to hear it. I *need* to hear it."

Lorna is again silent, but then looks up into his eyes. Her hands are drooped lifeless in her lap. She appears defeated.

"Jeremiah, it's not a woman thing. It's just that ... that, you don't know me, even after all these many years. We exchange surface stuff to each other, but inside, inside me, you know nothing of my past, things that I ...

"You probably think I'm just a naïve, small town country bumpkin, livin' in the 'sticks' and all, but you're wrong. You're *dead* wrong!  There are some things a girl, a woman, anyone, just doesn't talk about.  Or even want to think about!"

She gets up and continues, staring down Bedloe with hands now stiffly at her side, fists clenched tightly.  With her voice trembling, tears cloud her vision.  She looks terrified for some reason.

"What that man did to his daughter was beyond evil.  You probably have a word for it, but I don't.  But I know the word here," and puts a quivering hand over her heart.  "And, here," and hits her stomach hard with the other hand still clinched in a fist.

"Lorna," he leans against the wall, "what if there was something that prevented him from ..."

She snaps back before he has time to finish the question.

"Oh, for the love of Jesus, don't start giving me psychological bull crap!  *He raped his daughter!*  That could've been *your* daughter, Sarah.  My daughter, Amelia.  My ..."

She sits down hard on her chair.

Bedloe is attempting to understand, but is now a bit befuddled.

"This conversation is going to get us absolutely nowhere fast.  I haven't even looked over the case yet.  It's Thursday.  Swain isn't coming back in until Monday, right?  But, I'll tell you this right here and now.  If I decide to take it after I learn all I can, and if Swain can retain me, I swear, on both our daughter's names, I'll share everything with you beforehand."

Lorna gets up again and walks to the big window overlooking downtown La Crosse. Once there, she stops to look through the ice-covered glass into the frozen February sky.

"And, I swear to you, if you go ahead with this, then I have to make a decision as well."


Jeremiah Bedloe is walking home after the day's work, and despite the cold, his pace is slow. His thoughts are still of Lorna. Snow is falling, the air is calm. Cass Street is quiet and deserted, the crunch of his overshoes on the sidewalk's ice and rock salt is clearly heard. It is peaceful.

Once in his apartment, he fixes himself a hamburger. After putting some French fries in the microwave, he cuts a slice of sweet onion and puts it and some ketchup onto a bun, then prepares his brandy on the rocks. When the bachelor meal is ready, he picks up both the plate and glass, and proceeds to the little table in the living room.

Again, the briefcases catch his eye, still sitting near the desk.

"The only way I'm going to find out, is to read what the hell's in there."

After finishing his meal, Bedloe goes to the desk and turns one of the briefcases upside down, emptying the contents onto the desktop.

The telephone rings.

"Hello."

"Jeremiah?"

"Yeah. Who is it?"

"Michael Swain."

"Your timing is impeccable."

"I hope you don't mind my calling you at home."

"Why would I? I gave you one of my cards with the number on it."

"I was just wondering if you've had the time to read anything yet."

"No, I just dumped everything out of one briefcase. But, I've got to tell you, I have no idea where to start. Give me a hint. Is there some order to all this?"

"Well, I think you should start with the paper I wrote. Can I ask a question?"

"Go ahead."

"Have you ever heard of Klinefelter syndrome, or something called 47, XXY?"

"I noticed them in your writings. What are they? Is it important?"

"Yes, very important. It's a sex chromosomal disorder – males with an extra X chromosome. It's genetic. Listen, it's hard to explain, especially over the phone. Please concentrate on that in my report. It's very thorough. It should answer some questions you may have about whether or not we have a possible case here, and if you will represent my son. Then read all the medical reports, especially the one from the MidState Medical Center. That will *definitely* be an eye-opener."

Bedloe responds. "Your next appointment is Monday. I'll look this stuff over and have a decision for you then. We also have to talk about a retainer, so think about that. If I take the case, it won't be cheap, you should know that right up front. Along with my fee, we'll probably end up paying for experts to testify about all this. We're then in the neighborhood of fifty thousand, minimum."

There's an expected silence at the other end of the telephone. Swain replies. "I understand. I'll see you Monday. Thank you."


A definite chill permeates the office on Friday, and one not associated with weather. Very little is said, and the silence is emphatic. Both Jeremiah Bedloe and Lorna Dunn have made their positions clear, and it is evident neither of them is going to back down.

In order to spare his secretary and himself the grief, the briefcases stay in his apartment. However, she's certainly aware of why they're not in the office. After so many years in his employ, she realizes his interest in this case is growing each day. He doesn't have to say a word about it, Lorna simply knows.

That evening, Victor and Lorna sit at their dining room table at the usual hour. Prior to leaving for La Crosse that morning, she put a seasoned venison roast in the slow-cooker, along with carrots, potatoes, and Brussels sprouts – all picked from their garden and canned during the summer. By the time they both get home from work in the late afternoon, the aroma is magnificent. Lorna told her husband of Michael Swain and his son the night before, but it was only discussed briefly, then quickly dropped.

They eat silently, not looking up at each other. Victor is especially consumed by the entrée. Finally, after five minutes or so, he speaks.

"Lorn', this roast's a dilly. Tender. Must be from a doe. Or did ya do this one different, eh?"

Lorna slowly picks at the same meal and doesn't respond. Victor asks another question.

"Where's Amelia?"

"She's at basketball practice. You should *know that by now!*"

"Jeez, woman, bite my head off."

She shrugs her shoulders.

"Sorry, Hon', she should be getting home soon. Supper'll still be warm."

"You ain't hardly touching yours, Lorn'. What's the deal?"

"Victor, you know what the *deal* is."

46

There's an uncomfortable silence. He puts the knife and fork down.

"You never told him – didn't tell him today what got you so riled up."

She shakes her head, still picking at the food.

"He's been 'around the horn' a couple times, you know. You ain't gonna shock him. Maybe he needs to know."

"That's all got nothing to do with nothing."

Victor shrugs his shoulders and goes back to eating.

"I suppose. Anyway, you know best."

"No, Victor, I don't know best!"

She slams the knife and fork hard against the table.

"And I get tired of people saying that!"

Victor matches anger with anger, reciprocating by slamming *his* utensils onto the table in the same manner.

"*Woman*, how long you gonna carry this dang thing around inside ya all by yourself? *How long*? Heck, even I probably don't know half of it. And I'm your dad-gum *husband*, don't you know?"

"I'm not carrying nothing. Let's just finish supper in peace. I don't want to talk about it. Please."

"Then eat, for heaven's sake."

When the meal is completed, Lorna and Victor go into the living room to watch television.  As is their nightly week-day routine, they sit together on the sofa couch watching the five o'clock local news from La Crosse, and then the national evening news.

They hear their daughter's voice behind them.  "Hi mom." "Hi daddy."

Victor beats Lorna to respond.

"Hi sweetie, how was practice?"

"Okay.  What smells so good?  I'm hungrier than heck."

Lorna stares lovingly at her daughter for a moment, and then responds softly.

"A roast.  In the Crock-Pot.  Should be warm enough.  Let me know if it isn't."

"Thanks."

Amelia goes into the kitchen to eat and the couple's concentration returns to the television set.  After about a minute or two, Lorna abruptly states in a quiet voice, still looking straight ahead:

"I told Jeremiah, in so many words, that if he takes this case ... I'm through.  I ... I can't do it."  She starts to cry.

Victor continues to stare at the screen and thinks about responding but doesn't, except to take his wife's hand into his, patting it gently with the other in loving concern.

That same evening, Jeremiah Bedloe is at his apartment desk. Cheap Walmart reading glasses hang just above the tip of his nose. The desk is filled with the contents of both briefcases.

At nine-thirty, he stops reading and leans back in his chair. He slowly swirls his brandy-on-the-rocks in his hand, and the ice ricocheting off the glass makes a deliciously comforting sound of quiet contentment.

After another sip, he places the drink on the desk, takes off the eye glasses, and puts one stem between his lips. Deep in thought, he simultaneously rubs the inner corners of his eyes with thumb and index finger.

Bedloe puts the glasses back on and picks up the MidState Medical Center report, scanning a couple of pages before abruptly throwing it back down on the desk. He's getting tired.

Despite his fatigue, he grabs hold of Michael Swain's report, totally enthralled and spellbound by it all. Key words and thoughts fill his mind.

*Only one extra X chromosome. Klinefelter. All the research. The disorders because of it. The law versus genetics. The court cases, throughout the world. The judges' decisions. Prison terms. So many. The parents, again, all over the world. The same story, different people. What they go through. I had no idea.*

Then, Bedloe picks up the transcript of the court sentencing hearing of September 10, 2010 and turns to the prosecutor's questioning of the forensic psychologist. It's almost as if Bedloe is there at the hearing, listening to them as they banter back and forth, rather casually, about the overwhelming number of psychological disorders that affect Russell Swain. It seems he had so many. *But did he?*

Bedloe senses they weren't even dealing with this man's life.

*It was like Swain wasn't even there. The significance of the multitude was all ignored, replaced with bureaucratic, legal bullshit.*

*The judge. The prosecutor. The little town of Cambridge. The court's findings. The victim impact statement given by the victim's mother. No facts, just hidden emotions and biases. And no defense. Then the sentence.*

Bedloe once again picks up the MidState Medical Center report and stares at it.

*Medications. All in one year. All at the same time. Street drugs. Didn't they know what they were doing? What it could lead to?*

He leans back and looks to the ceiling.

*The history of this man. Failure. Does he know why? If he doesn't, he's not alone. No one knows, including me. Every time he had it good, he screwed it up. Now warehoused. Out of the way. Yet, his father says that he's at peace. Content. Does he want to be in prison? Why? Escape?*

*The victim, Russell Swain's daughter, lying there vulnerable and violated. The thought of it, the thought of doing such a horrid thing to her. Yet, what of me? Am I immune? If I were this man, and in his condition? What if I were him?*

## Scene Five

# Lorna's Secret

*The following Monday morning, February 20, 2012. Jeremiah Bedloe rides the elevator to his office floor.*

Depleted of energy, the emotional rollercoaster that prefaced the decision whether or not to take the Russell Swain case was unequalled in his career.

The weekend was spent dissecting every aspect of the case he could find or think of, and the plan he would need to follow if he decides to defend this man.

Bedloe has lived in the Upper Mississippi River Basin long enough to know that if he goes ahead with it, many people will turn their backs on him. But, as always, he feels that's the least of his concerns.

The thing is, it's such a "hot-button" issue and a crime too sordid for the majority of people to avoid letting prejudice cloud their thinking, especially considering the victim was a child.

The elevator opens and he walks down the corridor to the office, fighting off an uncharacteristic pessimism that invades his thinking. For the first time, he's second-guessing a decision he's already made.

How could he find an objective jury in this part of the country?  Or even a jury that would be able to understand it all. Especially in Minnesota.  He laughs inside at his own biased and prejudicial thinking, yet not questioning its validity.

He contemplates the complexities of the law at battle with a defense based on genetics and mental disorders.  Any defense attorney who wades into such a case as a father raping his daughter because of these reasons, is risking not just a defeat, but becoming a laughing stock among his peers for even attempting such folly.  The history in the courts definitely favors the law.

Yet, there is more to the State of Minnesota v. Russell Howard Swain than anyone is aware of.  Because of this, despite the odds, Bedloe is excited and ready to begin the challenge of proving this man's innocence.


His thoughts turn to Lorna as he reaches his law office door, still unsure why she reacted in such a way.  His secretary has been through a lot of cases with him, some almost as distasteful as this.

Surprisingly, the door is locked so he takes out his key and opens it, thinking she accidently locked it from inside.  When he walks in, his secretary is not at her desk.  Bedloe walks to the coat closet.  It's empty.

"What the hell's going on?  She was going to wait until I decided."

"Good morning, JB. Went out for the Trib'. It wasn't delivered."

Lorna looks around the office.

"Who are you talking to?"

He's relieved and responds rather meekly.

"Nobody. Myself."

He laughs inside, aware of the subconscious response.

Lorna takes off her winter garments and hangs them on hooks in the coat closet. Bedloe follows and does the same. His secretary stands near her desk, astounded.

"Miracles never cease."

"Yeah, well, I'm trying to turn over a new leaf. Never too old, or too late, so they say."

Bedloe nervously walks into his office, wondering if the woman is again right on his heels. He reaches the desk and turns to sit down. She's nowhere in sight.

After a few minutes, he courageously shouts out, "When's Swain coming in?"

There's a momentary silence.

"One-thirty."

"Okay."

Lorna soon enters Bedloe's office and stops just inside the door. She leans against the door frame with arms folded and scans the area, clearly disturbed and challenging her boss to level with her.

"Where're the briefcases?"

He sheepishly responds with a half-truth.

"Still in my apartment. There was no reason to bring them back yet."

"Really? Even though Mr. Swain has the appointment."

She shakes her head and abruptly turns to leave. Bedloe follows her.

"Lorna, is there anything you want to tell me? I'm not a novice when it comes to controversy, you know."

"I know."

She doesn't offer any more. Her voice now appears unemotional, which matches her expression. Any questions or responses are going to continue being very brief. However, for some reason, tears fill her eyes.

Bedloe returns to his office and sits down. He rhythmically taps his fingers on the desk top for a while, then stands up again. He goes to sit in a chair where clients wait, facing Lorna.

"This is one of the reasons why I've endured two divorces. I could never adapt to silence as a weapon."

"It's not a weapon."

"I would never expect a woman to concede that it is."

He smiles and she reciprocates with an uncommon sneer.

"Where are we going with this, JB?"

"You know I've made a decision."

She nervously leans back in her chair, arms again folded on her chest.

"Yes."

Bedloe goes on. "I ask one thing before telling you what I've decided."

"What?" Despite her one word responses, Lorna's voice is clearly quivering with emotion.

"That you tell me why you got so upset last week. The look on your face when Swain unloaded was a very disturbing sight to see. I wanted to come out and ask you then. Perhaps I should have. Maybe the door should've been closed right away. But that's hindsight. You heard it all."

He continues, aware she is now close to crying.

"Lorna, we've been through one hell of a lot together for all these years. At times, you've stood by me when almost everyone else didn't. We only exchange 'surface stuff?' Hell, that's not true, and you know it. We're not only employee-employer, but friends. We're different though, and always have been. You and I are from different worlds, yet, in many ways, we're the same. But, you've got your life, as it is, and I've got mine ... as it is. We may go our own separate way once we leave here, but that's okay. In the office, we're a team."

He joins his hands together, fingers interlaced.

Lorna looks down, her eyelids seeming to flutter. Her voice is subdued.

"Jeremiah, this one's personal. Too much so. Yes, we're different. We learned over the years not to get involved in each other's lives. Some things were none of my business, and now, some are none of yours. They're best-left-be."

She continues, now making occasional eye contact.

"I could easily make a list of things I've heard others accused you of. Only you know. None of it had anything to do with my job or this office, so I let it go. I ask you now to do the same."

"But this one *did* have something to do with the office, Lorna. Not once have I seen you react like that. And then giving me that ultimatum?"

He shakes his head in a quandary, and then continues.

"What that man did to his daughter was ... I *don't* have a word for it. It was too awful. But, more importantly, his behavior deeply affects *you* for some reason. I want to know why that is. I need to know."

Bedloe is through talking, and waits for her to respond. If she doesn't, he knows what his secretary's going to do.

Lorna turns away, gazing at nothing in particular, recalling her husband's words. Bedloe feels tension within her, with emotions building stronger in his employee and dear friend.

There are no appointments this morning, so she stiffly walks to the office entrance door leading to the hallway, locks it, pulls down the shade, and then returns to sit. Bedloe sees a stern, flat expression on her face, devoid of all emotion.

Lorna's eyes penetrate Bedloe's but doesn't see him. She again looks away with eyelids slowly closing, her entire body now trembling. A transformation progresses rapidly and it is haunting.

Her expressions are changing, becoming twisted and frightening as long suppressed thoughts are dragged up to consciousness.

Then, emotional recollections of events long past verbally come forth, angrily, yet calmly.

As she speaks, no tears escape her still closed eyes. Her expression doesn't change. However, an occasional grin sadistically strikes out and seeks revenge.

Bedloe sees that the woman is so in pain he wants her to stop, but he remains silent, needing to hear her. He sits stunned, his face flushes with embarrassment.

These things happen to other people, not to someone he knows. Someone he cares about, and in his own way, loves.


The devastation endured when a young girl ten years of age, the unthinkable evil that ripped and gutted her of all innocence.

Lorna shared a second-floor bedroom with her fourteen-year old sister, Emma. Nights when their father came home drunk, which was often, he'd go directly to Emma and aggressively rip off her nightgown and panties. Then, he'd quickly take off his bib overalls and underwear, and mounted his daughter.

When these perverted episodes started, she'd fight the painful attack, but soon learned to succumb to what was occurring, and waited for her father to finish. All the while, Lorna and her sister stared at each other, while their mother remained downstairs sobbing, knowing that any attempt to stop this pernicious assault on her beautiful child, would result in a severe beating to all, or even death.

Finally, after months of the desecrating behavior, her beloved sister terminated the pain. She took her own life and was forever in the loving and protective arms of the Lord.

The adult child sits in silence, motionless and quiet for a while. Bedloe thinks her recollections of this dreadful experience have concluded – they haven't. She continues.

Weeks after her sister's funeral, late at night, the father came for Lorna as she slept. This time the mother had to respond. She stood blocking his path to the bed and screamed: *"Enough. For the love of God, enough."* He viciously hit his wife with a fist, sending her to the floor, unconscious. Lorna was awake and saw it all, terrified he'd killed her.

The girl then looked up in horror as her father approached the bed. She knew what was about to happen. Breaking his only remaining child from a protective fetal position, she fought the attack, but the futile attempt only further excited him.

His alcohol-laced breathing became heavier and louder, and hot guttural grunts echoed through the room as the rape persisted. He continued to cause her excruciating pain while she wept in childhood surrender, trying to think of anything to take her away from what was happening.

Lorna looks at Bedloe and gives him a cold smile, and then resumes her description of the ordeal.

Her mother regained enough consciousness to crawl to the first floor and telephone her brother. He and another brother immediately came over with deer rifles and a rope, ending the vile behavior they were witnessing.

Head-butted with one of the rifles, the brothers pulled him off their niece. His blood gushed and immediately soaked throughout the bed sheets, covering Lorna as well. They forced a handkerchief deep into her father's throat to keep him silent. Semiconscious, with his hands tied behind him, his bloodied naked body was carried out of the house. It was the last time Lorna, or anyone else, ever saw him again.

No one in the town questioned his whereabouts, including the sole village police officer or the county sheriff's department. Everyone simply went about their business and

Lorna was to later understand – what was done to her father was just and the right thing to do.

Rumor has it he was shot dead in an open field, an anvil then rope-tied to his waist, and his body was dumped somewhere in the Mississippi River.

Throughout her story, Lorna's voice progressively rises in pitch, speaking and appearing now almost as a child. She stares at the ceiling.

"Mommy died the next year of a broken heart and guilt for not having saved my sister and me, I kind of guess. My being born and raised on a farm outside Lansing was a fib, a … a lie. I'm sorry. We lived in a little town down river 'bout two hundred miles or so, I think. 'Don't even know the name now.

"When mommy died, I was all alone. Uncle Billy moved me to Lansing to live with my Auntie Clara from my daddy's side. She's a good woman, who knew of her brother. She still lives there in Lansing, and you'll *never* get her to say a word about any of this."

Lorna looks pleadingly at her employer with wide, scarlet red eyes. "Please, you've got to swear. You've got to swear!"

Promptly, Lorna lapses into an almost catatonic state as Bedloe searches for words to comfort her. Tears run down his face as he gets up to telephone Victor. Then, quietly hanging up the phone, the attorney places a hand gently on her shoulder, and immediately feels her muscles tighten and shrug it away. He returns to the chair and sits down. No words are exchanged, however, their eyes fix on one another.

After a while, Victor and Amelia arrive to take their loved one home. Bedloe goes to unlock the door and raises the shade. Her winter garments on and ready to leave, Lorna tightly grasps her husband's arm, while Amelia's arm is draped over her shoulders. As Lorna walks to the door, she stops and speaks to Bedloe – in normal voice without turning.

"I will pray for you tonight. Don't know what I'm going to do, but I do know this. You wouldn't take something unless you felt it was right.

"You're a good man, Jeremiah Bedloe. A good man."

Victor opens the door and they leave. Bedloe quietly closes it behind them, staring at his trembling hand on the door knob.


He goes into his office and slumps loudly into his chair. Having watched and listened while this kind and common adult woman completely emptied her soul of a dormant burden that had obviously haunted her life for so long, he questions the wisdom of having been a party to its resurrection.

Bedloe rubs open hands hard against his face to wipe away the tears, while simultaneously shaking his head back and forth. Both are an attempt to blot out feelings of regret, and what he had just witnessed.

At twenty-seven minutes past one, Michael Swain stands just inside the outer door to the law office. He sees no one sitting at Lorna's desk, so signals his arrival with a loudly whispered question.

"Hello, is anyone here?"

Bedloe walks out of his office.

 "Yeah."

"Did I get the day and time right?"

"You're right on time. Come on in."

Swain follows Bedloe into the office and sits. Bedloe walks to his chair and sits as well. He picks up a piece of paper from the desk, however his hand is shaking so obviously, he immediately puts it down. His voice is hoarse.

"You'll have to forgive me … it's been … kind of a bad day."

Swain doesn't respond. Bedloe nervously makes little eye contact.

"I looked over your stuff … the papers you wrote and the documents you copied. It was pretty overwhelming … to say the least."

Bedloe stops talking for reasons unknown to Swain, and appears in a state of suspension. After a moment, he resumes speaking in short spurts, still with no eye contact.

"You obviously did a lot of work … put a lot of time on all that. But … from a legal standpoint … I really don't know …

don't know what we can do.  There are several issues we can … pursue, but the question … the question is …"

Swain interrupts.

"Excuse me, there's something wrong."

"Wrong?"

Bedloe's mind is still with Lorna and he can't think of anything else.  He looks up at Swain.

"Listen, where are you staying?"

"I've got a nice motel room on the north side."

"My secretary had a very emotional experience today and, to be quite honest, I'm tired and beat because of it as well.  Would you mind if we do this tomorrow morning, say at eleven?  Would it be putting you out too much?"

"Certainly not."

Swain looks at Bedloe, now sensing what the problem may be.  He needs to determine whether or not to make a particular statement, a very sensitive one.  He decides to proceed.

"Jeremiah, when I was telling you about my son Russ the other day, I could almost feel some static, an anger coming at me from your secretary.  When I turned to apologize for using a curse word, something was dreadfully wrong with her."

He continues, carefully.

"Like I mentioned to you before, I was a counselor at the college, and a therapist of sorts. To the students and their families. For a long time."

He hesitates in thought, and then adds the statement.

"Your secretary, she's a victim. Or directly involved with a victim."

Bedloe looks at the man but doesn't respond. Swain concludes with a question.

"If my son is your client, will it create a problem?"

"No."

## Scene Six

# The Prison Meeting

*The next day, Tuesday morning.*

Bedloe awakens well past sunrise, goes to the kitchen for a tall glass of milk to sooth his still troubled stomach, then takes a hot shower and shaves. He dries his hair thoroughly, dresses, and walks to work feeling refreshed. Inexplicable to anyone other than him, the nightly consumption of brandy was eliminated the previous night.

Arriving at the Hoeschler Building a little before nine, by habit, Bedloe expects to see Lorna at her desk. Instead, he is greeted with the unaccustomed silence of an empty solitary office. Remembering there are no appointments until Swain's at eleven, he picks up the La Crosse Tribune outside the door, then walks to a restaurant on Fourth Street for breakfast. He sits quietly eating while reading the local news.

Returning to the office, a melancholic longing to see his secretary troubles him, but he rejects it because there's work to be done. At his desk, he calls a car rental agency in La Crosse and makes a reservation for the next morning.

At eleven a.m., Michael Swain arrives for his appointment. Bedloe is sitting in Lorna's chair, looking for something in one of her desk drawers. He looks up.

"As is quite apparent, I've been demoted. Actually, some critics would say it's a promotion."

Swain laughs. "I'll let you be the judge of that."

They go into Bedloe's office and take their customary seats. He gestures to the briefcases that are sitting nearby.

"Well, like I said yesterday, I spent a good portion of last weekend looking over the contents of those briefcases – the papers you wrote and all the printed stuff.

"From a legal standpoint, this'll be one hell of a battle right from the start and all the way to the end. There are several issues we can possibly pursue, but the question is, in what order. And, I really don't know yet what you're specifically going after."

Swain assertively informs Bedloe. "I want my son free to get professional help. That's all I want. If Russ is free and doesn't get it done, then I'm through with it, and he'll probably end up back in the slammer. I've got to move on with my life."

Bedloe nods his understanding.

"Okay, I get it. So what you're after is not so much a downward departure of sentence, but a complete release so he can get into treatment and counseling." The attorney writes it on his legal pad and then continues.

"One of the major stumbling blocks right from the get-go is that damn guilty plea back in 2010. We can't start over. The two subsequent appeals submitted by the public defender's office after he went to prison were denied as well. No big surprise."

He thinks and Swain waits.

"I asked you before if you'd ever heard of *diminished capacity.* Have you?"

"No."

"Minnesota doesn't recognize it, but it could possibly be used."

"What is it?"

"It's a potential defense by which a defendant argues that, although he or she broke the law and was judged guilty, they should not be held fully liable criminally for doing so, because their mental functioning was diminished by circumstances beyond his or her control. In other words, they weren't fully responsible. It's a slim possibility but may be worth pursuing.

"Generally, it states that if your son suffered a mental disease which did not enable him to appreciate the consequences of his actions, or didn't know what he was doing was wrong, he should not be held accountable."

Swain looks puzzled. "But Russ *knows* what he did."

"You're right. The question is not so much the mental diseases the prosecutor and forensic psychologist randomly rummaged through at the sentencing hearing, but the drugs, the medications. That wasn't brought up at all. As far as I can tell, no one knows about that other than you, me, your son, and the clinic.

"How much effect did they have? That's the key. Where a plea has to be based on some form of mental abnormality, it need not only involve insanity. Courts have included any condition brought on by the consumption of drink or drugs, and even food."

"Food?"

Bedloe nods. "But these situations involved murders, that ended up with the court reducing the charge to manslaughter. We'd have to show that your son's case should be included in this and that he be freed to get into therapy. You ever heard of the 'Twinkie defense?'"

"Twinkie? No."

The attorney stands and starts walking behind his desk while Swain follows him with his eyes.

"It was in San Francisco in the late seventies, and it involved the first openly gay member of the board of supervisors, Harvey Milk. The accused, a guy by the name of Dan White, shot to death two men, the mayor and Milk. White's attorney argued diminished capacity.

"They claimed a diet of only junk food had created a chemical imbalance in White's brain, and that he was also depressed over the loss of his city job. The combination of the two resulted in him murdering the two officials. Therefore, he was unable to form the thoughts constituting premeditation, one of the requirements for a first-degree murder conviction.

"Based on diminished capacity, the jury convicted him of voluntary manslaughter, the least serious charge for a murder. The bad news is that, shortly afterwards, outraged by the verdict, the San Francisco voters forced the California legislature to throw out this defense. It's got a bad reputation in a lot of jurisdictions, including Minnesota. But, several court cases around the country have recently used it, not for a 'not guilty' plea, but for a reduced sentence."

"Do you think my son would fit into this?"

"I don't know. Could be, but don't get your hopes up. Again, Minnesota doesn't recognize this plea. Attorneys there have tried using it, but to my knowledge, haven't been successful.

"Yet, just the fact that they tried, gives me hope it may be possible. Why would they do that, knowing it was futile going in? It wouldn't make sense.

"The key here are the drugs prescribed for your son. And, his disorders. But, this particular plea differs in important ways from 'not guilty by reason of insanity,' which aims for a verdict of 'not guilty' and sends the looney to a mental institution. No offense."

The father quickly responds, smiling. "None taken. I'm starting to understand your personality."

Bedloe sits back into his chair and nods.

"What we'd be asking the court is that, based on the medical and psychological stuff you've found, your son's guilty plea be waived and that he be granted a trial for the same offense." He looks dead serious at Swain.

"Also, Michael, you've got to be realistic. The bottom-line is that the jury may only consider a downward departure from sentencing guidelines.  We'll go for the total release but may have to settle for a reduced sentence."

Swain reacts disturbingly.

"No.  Like I said a few minutes ago, I want him *released*, free, to get the right kinds of treatment."

"What'd you mean by the right kinds of treatment?"

"If we go after a reduced sentence, the prison system will end up doing the therapy.  Their sex-offender treatment program is a *joke* and has never rehabilitated anyone. Minnesota state legislators and the press have both stated publicly, it's a bureaucratic waste of the tax payer's money.

"As for Klinefelter syndrome, the Director of Health Services for the Minnesota Department of Corrections stated to me that Russ is getting the appropriate treatment in prison. But he isn't, because there are no doctors in Minnesota who know anything about it.  Especially treating *adults*."

"Can you prove all that?"

"Yes.  It's in the briefcases."

Bedloe grins and shakes his head.

"The briefcases again.  I should've known.  So, the first monumental challenge is to get a trial by jury.  Since he pleaded guilty, was sentenced in district court, and lost on appeal, that's going to be tough.  I'll definitely have to go before the Minnesota Court of Appeals for that one."

Bedloe goes back into deep thought and then asks:

"Did you bring your computer from Florida?"

Swain nods. "Yes."

"Good. What's that called, 'wire-less?' Can you hook that up at the motel?"

"It's already done."

"Okay. Bone up on some of these things I'll be telling you. Read about them. Use your educated brain to find relationships between, say, diminished capacity and the drugs. And also that Klinefelter thing.

"I've never done this before, but because of the case's uniqueness and complexity, and perhaps because I'm a tad looney myself, I'm going to use you as kind of an assistant. I'll work on the legal aspects of the case, relying on you to cover the psychological and medical. Will you do that?"

"Certainly."

Bedloe gets up again and slowly paces back and forth around the office in deep thought, simultaneously shaking his head and tapping a pencil against his open hand.

"There's a hell of a lot a jury may have to absorb, but together, we may be able to convince them." He stops and looks at Swain. "Like I said, it's a long shot."

Swain explains what has to be done up here if he doesn't go back down south.

"I'll have to rearrange things in Florida, someone to take care of my house and some other matters. I might have to make a couple of trips to check things out, especially during hurricane season."

The defense attorney is silent and still for a moment.

"Come to think of it, everything I need from you can be done in Florida. When's hurricane season?"

"Not until June first, and it goes until the end of November."

"Hell, I'm hoping this'll be over by then."

Swain looks at Bedloe, a little anger creeping into his demeanor. "Jeremiah, one thing still bothers the hell outa me. Russ' defense lawyer at the court sentencing hearing didn't use any of what I found, and it was easily available to him!"

"Forget about that. Anyway, I found his name in the hearing transcript and called him last Saturday morning." Then Bedloe gets angry himself. "He wanted your son to plead not guilty and have a trial by jury, knowing the reputations of the judges and prosecutors involved. If Russell would've listened to him, chances are we wouldn't be here today."

Swain is now deeply angered. "That may be true, but then he didn't have to go and feed my son to those county blood-thirsty 'lions.' The son-of-a-bitch took twenty-grand of Russ' teacher retirement fund and split the scene. The lazy bastard was so morally inept, a legal precedence from 1906 was the only defense used in the whole goddamned case!"

Bedloe nods and moves on, smiling at Swain's spunk.

"Okay, one last thing. Contact everyone you know involved in the Klinefelter thing and tell them what we're doing. You've got to get them to state whether or not they'll support us. It's one thing to have all this stuff you found, but they have to stand and deliver when we need them to testify. It all has to be on the record.

"I need a list of the Klinefelter big wigs you've contacted, with their addresses and current phone numbers, then I'll have Lorna ..." – he glances at his secretary's empty chair in the other room.

"I'll handle it," Swain says quickly.

Bedloe gets back on track. "Like I said earlier, I have to go before the Minnesota appellate court and plead your son's case, using what's called a 'post-conviction relief petition.' It all starts there. Essentially, it is a motion to withdraw that guilty plea based on new evidence, and if granted, he would have the right to a trial by jury on the charges originally filed against him. Without that, the case dies."

He shakes his head. "I'm still concerned about that Klinefelter thing. I don't know, I keep questioning its seriousness in your son. It just seems a little iffy. Our chances seem better just going after the drugs."

Swain responds. "Jeremiah, you keep on calling it, 'that Klinefelter thing.' In all the reading I've done and the people I've talked to for two years now, it clearly shows that most of the problems Russ has, plus all the drugs given to him, directly or indirectly resulted from his being 47, XXY, having Klinefelter syndrome. There's *definitely* a connection between the two."

"Maybe. But who knows that? You and about sixteen other people in this country. I don't know if we can get a jury to buy it. Hell, you said yourself, you didn't know 'dick' about this Klinefelter thing – Klinefelter *syndrome* until recently, and the only reason was because your son has the disease."

"It's not a disease, it's a genetic disorder."

"Whatever."

Swain doesn't let it go.

"*No*, it's not *whatever*. Look, a disease is most often something you acquire in life, but a genetic disorder is something you're *born* with. To my way of thinking, Russ has a chance of getting rid of an acquired disease, but will be 47, XXY all his life and needs to understand it and be treated for it."

Bedloe looks respectfully at Swain, smiling.

"You keep things like that firmly in mind. That's the kind of stuff we need."

"Jeremiah, we haven't talked about the retainer."

"You're right, we haven't. Well, my friend, perhaps I've got a late Christmas gift for you. If the appellate court accepts our petition for a jury trial, and we *go* to trial, it won't cost you a dime."

"How's that?"

"We're going after the MidState Medical Center, with a lawsuit seeking monetary damages. Their reports convinced me as soon as I read them to go pro bono. I haven't figured out the dollar figure in the lawsuit yet, but it'll be steep. Whatever your son receives, my cut is forty per cent. If he gets nothing, I get nothing. Take it or leave it."

Swain doesn't hesitate.

"I'd be a fool not to take it."

"You're right. And, so would Russell. I already called the prison at Moose Lake. I need to spend some time with your son and get to know him. I'm going there tomorrow."

"Maybe I could go along."

"No. This has got to be one on one. We're going to get down and dirty. You'll just be in the way. Understand?"

Swain nods. Bedloe continues. "Good. I don't need you to do anything right now. You might want to think about going down south until I hear what the court decides. We'll keep discussing the case by phone, unless I decide you should come back up north."

"Jeremiah, thank you."

"I hope to hell you'll still thank me when all this is over."


*The next day, Wednesday, two p.m.*


Bedloe waits in a small office adjacent to the visiting area of the Moose Lake Correctional Facility in Moose Lake,

Minnesota. The drive, which is 202 miles due north of La Crosse, took a little over three and a half hours. He's exhausted from the ride in the small rental car and didn't stop for lunch – now wishing he would had.

After a ten-minute wait, a guard walks in with a tall, large man with short black hair and a very deep receding hairline atop a pear-shaped head. The attorney is shocked at the lack of any father-son resemblance, almost to the point he doubts they are related or that the guard brought out the wrong man.

Russell is wearing a prison-issue T-shirt that doesn't hide a granite torso. Bedloe is thinking, compared to his father, who is of average height and weight, this guy has got to be at least six-four, and weigh two-hundred and thirty pounds of solid muscle. Bedloe has never seen a mug shot of what the obese Russell Swain looked like when he was booked into the Isanti County Jail in 2010.

As their eyes meet, Swain's smile is contagious and there is a quiet, confident aura about him. They haven't spoken yet but Bedloe is a master at reading people simply by their presence and demeanor.

"Russell, Jeremiah Bedloe," he says, extending his right hand.

Swain takes the attorney's smaller hand in his and shakes it politely. However, Bedloe immediately confirms the authentic strength behind the man's carefully controlled grip.

"It's a pleasure meeting you, sir."

"You appear surprised to see me. Have you spoken with your father?

"Yes, sir. I called him this morning. I knew he had contacted a lawyer but I'm basically unaware of what's going on. He cannot call me, so our communications are totally my doing. And the call can last no longer than fifteen minutes. But, he filled me in on some things."

"Well, I'm a defense attorney from La Crosse, licensed in both Wisconsin and Minnesota. Your father and I have been discussing your case quite thoroughly. I must say, he's quite a guy."

Russell reacts with a hearty boisterous laugh.

"You might say that."

Bedloe tells Swain what he proposes, explaining the procedures that must be followed and the length of time involved. He ends this part of their meeting by explaining the same pro bono arrangement he had given Russell's father – take it or Bedloe walks. Russell Swain takes it.

"Okay. Now, we only have about an hour and a half today to start discussing the history of what happened. I'll tell you right up front, no lying. You lie to me, I'll know it and then we're through. Do you understand?"

"Yes, sir."

"And call me Jeremiah."

"If you don't mind, I'd prefer calling you 'sir' or 'Mr. Bedloe.'"

"It's up to you.  One more thing before we start.  You need to be specific and provide me with all the details, no matter how gross or distasteful they may be.  Don't make me have to pry anything out of you.  That would be a waste of time for both of us.  Let's start with what happened."

Swain agrees, seemingly excited.  His enthusiasm appears almost childlike.  Bedloe reaches for his legal pad and pen.

"First of all, did you sexually assault your daughter?"

"Yes, sir."

"How many times?"

"Once."

"Do you remember the date?"

"It was January 2, 2010."

"How old was she when this occurred?"

"Twelve."

"Did you put a drug in her soft drink prior to raping her?"

Swain flinches at the word "rape".  Bedloe watches carefully.

"Yes, sir."

"Why?"

"To make her woozy."

"To increase the chances she'd submit?"

Swain hesitates. "Yes."

"Did she submit without a struggle?"

"She didn't struggle. I think she … she asked me not to do it."

"But you went ahead anyway," a statement more than a question.

Swain nods, looking at his hands. "Obviously."

"Do you love your daughter?"

"More than anything in the world." Tears form in his eyes.

"The heart tattoo on your arm there. Is that your daughter's name inside the heart?"

"Yes, sir."

"What's the date tattooed below it?"

"It's her birthday."

"How old was she when you were tattooed?"

He responds with emotion, "She was just born."

Bedloe continues to write in his legal pad as he goes on with the questioning.

"If your daughter were here today instead of me, what would you say to her?"

Swain is taken aback, and starts to cry.

"I'm sorry. Very sorry."

It doesn't faze Bedloe. He's concentrating on authenticity and sincerity.

"You pled guilty to this criminal offense. Why?"

"It was my understanding that if it'd gone to trial by jury, my daughter would've had to endure the whole thing, including being called to testify against me. I just wanted to spare her the pain and embarrassment of it all. I did it. I should be the only one punished." He wipes the tears with the back of his hand.

Bedloe continues. "But now, what? Has there been a change of heart? I'm soon going before the appellate court to try and get you a trial by jury. So, you've changed your mind about involving your daughter?"

"My dad said the trial would only involve the medications and Klinefelter syndrome. Not what I did, but why I did it."

"What do you think? Is that what caused the assault?"

Russell Swain doesn't answer right away. He thinks about the question for a moment.

"At the time, and before, I had no idea what the medications were doing to me. The doctors at the medical center explained the possibility of side effects but weren't very specific. I don't know anything about that stuff. I'm not a doctor. I only knew that the physical and mental problems I was having made me seek medical help, and they were handled with drugs. Because of my dad, today I know what they did to me."

"And what about Klinefelter?"

"I don't know much about that either, only what the doctors said years ago. My dad has been telling me about the psychological disorders involved with it. Also, we joined a national group out of Colorado, and they've been sending me stuff to read."

"Do you think Klinefelter syndrome caused you to assault your daughter?"

"Well, as my dad said ..."

"I didn't ask you what your dad said. What do *you* think?"

"I honestly don't know."

"Before going to prison, did you drink alcohol? Use 'pot'? Cocaine? Anything?"

"No."

"Never?"

"I gave it up in my thirties – alcohol and 'pot.'"

"How old are you now?"

"Forty-six."

Bedloe writes.

"How did the Isanti County Sheriff's Department find out about the assault?"

"I confessed it to my minister."

He looks up. "Your *minister?*"

"Yes, sir."

"Are you aware that clergy cannot be compelled to reveal confessions to the police without the confessor's permission?"

Swain nods his head.

Bedloe continues.

"So, you've heard of the Mandated Reporter Law."

"Yes, sir. My dad told me about it."

"Did you give the minister permission to call the sheriff's department?"

"No, sir. Pastor McCord didn't ask."

"Do you know why he found it necessary to immediately make the call?"

The attorney waits with his patented don't bullshit me facial expression. Swain looks down, shaking his head.

"I ... I confessed to him that ... I was having thoughts about having sex with my daughter again, and-and with my students. My dear God, I don't know what happened to me?"

Bedloe replies. "I'm working on that now. So, you had *thoughts* about your female students. What about behaviors?"

"Only thoughts."

"Moving on. Before the arrest, did you look at pornography?"

"Yes, sir." His head is still down.

"Often?"

"'Often' is a relative term."

"Alright, we'll do it your way. Daily?"

"Two or three times a week."

"That wasn't so hard, was it? DVDs? Pay-for-view? The internet?"

"The internet."

"What sort of stuff did you seek out and watch?"

"Name it."

"Sex with adults?"

"Yes."

"Homosexuality?

'Yes, occasionally."

"Bestiality, or sex with animals?"

"Just a little."

"Sadomasochism and bondage?"

Swain looks up to the ceiling, growing annoyed at the embarrassing questions. He gives out with a loud sigh. Bedloe questions why the man is responding this way, seeing he was so forthcoming with the ministers.

Swain responds.  "Hardly ever.  It was too violent and bloody."

"What about sex with children?"

"No."

He looks up from his legal pad.  "Did you say 'no?'"  Swain nods.

Bedloe doesn't pursue it for now, but knows this is a key point and will need clarification.


He then remembers reading in the court sentencing hearing transcript about Swain's detailed confessions to the ministers.

"Russell, it's striking that everything you watched on the internet, is identical to the behaviors you confessed to.  Did you both look at that stuff, and then act on them?"

"No, only looked.  I was mad at the ministers for not wanting me in the church mentor program, and wanted to get back at them.  So, it was all made up to sound like I actual did them."

"I don't understand why you'd do such a thing.  It ended up being included in all the county reports. The next prosecutor at a trial, like at the hearing in 2010, is going to have an arsenal of evidence to argue you had an unhealthy obsession with sordid sexual activities and viewing pornography.  He or she will say the medications and Klinefelter syndrome had nothing to do with it.  What do you say to that?"

"I don't have anything to say. After I was arrested, I told the forensic psychologist that all those things I said back then were lies, and that I'm strictly heterosexual with only adult women.

"The only thing I'm guilty of is watching too much porn, and the one act with my daughter. Nothing else."

Bedloe responds. "Whether it was true or not, you confessed to all that. Unfortunately, we have to live with it.

"So, what about now in prison? Like any normal guy, you must still have thoughts about sex."

"Yes. But since the arrest, God has entered my life and the Holy Spirit controls everything I do. He commands the demons to leave my soul and my mind."

"The Holy Spirit? Demons?"

"That's correct. I have given total authority to the Holy Spirit, and what He commands. He directs all our lives, and we will only know the inevitable glorious world to come, if we go to Him and abide by His holy laws."

Swain closes his eyes. "Mortals need not make decisions but simply wait for the Holy Spirit to guide and lead us in sacred and just paths on earth."

The attorney slowly shakes his head, buying none of it.

"Something like divine intervention?"

Swain opens his eyes and looks at Bedloe with what might be a bit of a snicker. "Something like that."

Jeremiah Bedloe, being an agnostic, wants terribly to challenge such unmitigated nonsense and level with his client about the destructive nature of such thinking, and what it can lead to. But he doesn't. Instead, he continues to listen to Swain's sermon, but can't keep himself from tossing in a quick comment once Swain is done.

"Have you ever heard the saying: 'There are no atheists in foxholes?'"

"No. What does it mean?"

"Never mind. What if this Holy Spirit commanded you to kill someone? Or sexually assault someone?"

Russell Swain looks offended, but answers calmly. "The Holy Spirit would never do that."

"Really? It's been known to happen."

"Only demons would make such a command. They've already tried and succeeded. But they will never do it again."

"What do you mean by, 'tried and succeeded?'"

"My dad didn't tell you?"

"Tell me what?"

"That night with my daughter, there were two demons in the room with us. I heard them but I know she didn't. She would've said something. They weren't physically present, as far as I could tell, but there were shadows and they whispered that what I was doing was good and should be done to her. They giggled and laughed as I did … what I did."

As he says it, he appears almost in a trance.

Swain is getting into a very bizarre area of disclosure. Bedloe learned many years ago from an FBI agent how to tell if someone's lying by watching their eyes while answering the question, and in which direction they look in relation to being left- or right-handed. If they look the opposite way, they're lying.

"Are you left- or right-handed?"

"Right. Why?"

He ignores the question. "Did you tell anyone else about this? Hearing demons?"

Swain looks directly at Bedloe. "Yes. Many people. Some I told months before that night with my daughter."

"Who?"

"My wife. Both ministers. I told my lawyer, the one I hired to get custody of my daughter. He told me not to say anything about it to anyone because if my first wife's lawyer found out, I'd never win custody."

"Wait a minute. Were you going for *permanent* custody of your daughter?"

"Yes."

When was this?"

"In 2009."

"How close were you to getting her?"

"Not very close. Her mother was battling it and putting me through hell."

"Did your daughter want to move in with you and your family?"

"Yes, more than anything. I was fixing up her own bedroom and was about to furnish it."

"Back to this *demon* thing. When did you tell your lawyer about that?"

"I don't know, about November of 2009, I think. A couple months before ..."

"What's his name? The lawyer."

"Tom Kraft. He's in Waseca."

Bedloe writes the name and city down on his legal pad.

"Anyone else?"

"The psychologist I was seeing, Janice Nelson. As a matter-of-fact, she called Kraft and said the demons were real. She's a faith-based Christian psychologist, and told him the demons had invaded me."

"Is that the reason she called him?"

"I have no idea."

"Where's her office?"

"Woodbury."

"What were you seeing her for?"

"ADHD and depression, also marital problems."

Bedloe continues to write. Swain remembers something else.

"Oh, and after I was arrested, the jail minister visited. I told him about the demons and that they were still with me. He suggested I conduct a *deliverance*, which he said is a strong religious command the demons leave."

"Did they?"

"No. Then he tried. They kept on whispering and giggling."

"Did the minister see or hear them?"

"No."

"Are they with you now?"

"No. I haven't been bothered by them for some time. When the Holy Spirit entered my life, protecting and guiding me, the demons left."

Bedloe writes down what Swain just said, then thinks for a few moments before proceeding. He is conflicted in bringing up the next subject because it is very controversial, especially in a court of law.

"Russell, I'd like to go back to the day of the assault and ask some pretty damn sensitive questions. As mentioned before, I don't want you lying. But, you're under no obligation to answer. I'm in your corner as long as there's honesty between us.  And for now, I'll take your word for it that all the demon stuff actually occurred in your mind."

Bedloe suddenly remembers he forgot to ask an obvious question.

"Before we continue, where was your wife and her kids the day of the assault?  They certainly weren't home."

"When we got back from Texas, they went to her folks' place in Alexandria to pick up the dog and visit for a spell.  It's about a two-hour trip from Cambridge."

"Got it.  Now, during your confessions and interviews with the sheriff's office after the arrest, you consistently gave the same account of what occurred.  I'd like to ask you some questions about that day."

"Mr. Bedloe, why are you asking this?  You've already read it all."

"I want to hear it straight from you.  To watch and listen. It's important if there's a trial, believe me.

"Now at the time, you had a load of stress going on in your life, right?"

"Yes."

"What was it caused by?"

"Fighting for custody of my daughter.  Also, I was called into the school principal's office and told there were four allegations of misconduct in the classroom.  She told me I was probably going to be fired.  Then ..."

"Were any of the allegations concerning sexual matters?"

"No." He goes on. "Also, there were marriage problems."

"Sexual problems? Were you two sexually active?"

Swain laughs to himself.

"We had no sexual problems. Let's just put it that way."

"Go on."

"Then, there was the depression because of the custody battle. Also, the ADHD and sleep apnea were causing problems."

"Were there medications for each?"

"Yes. Ambien for the sleep apnea, also Adderall and Vyvanse for the ADHD. And there were testosterone shots for Klinefelter syndrome. Along with all those, I was on citalopram for depression but took myself off it about July of that year. It made my whole body shake and my vision started to get worse. I could hardly drive."

"Were Ambien, Adderall, Vyvanse, and testosterone in your system the day of the assault?"

"All but Adderall. I was switched from that to Vyvanse. The Ambien was taken just before sitting down with my daughter to watch a movie, the Vyvanse an hour or two before that. The testosterone was ongoing, a shot every two weeks."

"Your wife stated that when you all flew home from Texas to Minnesota on the day of the assault, she was angered at you for taking an overdose of the sedative diazepam before boarding the plane."

"Yes. I think four pills, when I was only supposed to take two. Dumb. I was pretty scared about flying that day. The weather report said there were blizzard conditions in Minneapolis."

"How long after you took the diazepam did you arrive home?"

"About three hours, probably."

"That's the drug you put in your daughter's soft drink the day of the assault?"

"Yes."

"How many?"

"One."

Bedloe then goes on, now delving into the most sensitive part of the interview.

"Russell, take a deep breath. This may get ugly. According to what the record shows, on January 2, 2010, you were sitting side by side on the couch with your daughter watching a movie on the television."

"Yes." The lawyer continues.

"You told her all the stresses you were facing – the custody battle, your pending firing, health problems, and so on."

Swain again agrees, wondering what this is all leading to.

"Then, you started to sob heavily. Your daughter, feeling sorry for her dad, got up and sat on your lap."

Swain nods, momentarily unable to speak.

Bedloe goes on. "Did she sit on your lap sideways, kind of cuddling up to you?"

"No. She straddled me and hugged me real hard."

"Then what?"

"She … she kissed me."

"Like a father-daughter kiss?"

Swain looks out the window. "No."

He obviously doesn't want to stay on this subject.

"What happened then?"

"We held each other some more, and then something kind of clicked inside my head. I lost control. As best as I can recall, I asked her to take off her clothes. She did and then I took off mine." His face is beet red.

"Did she seem effected by the drug – slurred words and heavy eye-lids?"

Swain shakes his head, still gazing out the window.

"She slurred her words a little. That's about it, I think. I don't remember much about that day. It's still all a blur."

"Were the demons giggling and coaxing you on?"

He looks back at Bedloe. "Yes. That I know for sure."

"Then, according to what you told county sheriff's investigators and others, you both got up and went into the bedroom. Right?"

"Yes."

"The reports are conflicting concerning what happened next. Certain ones stated that, when the two of you were on the bed, she told you to stop, while others didn't mention that."

Bedloe leans back in his chair, intensely locked into his client's eyes.

"This whole damn thing really troubles me. I read over and over again the graphically explicit reports submitted by the two sheriff office special investigators who did the interrogation. They stated that both of you got on the bed, and it appeared what you were telling them was that your daughter participated in what was going on. Not consented, mind you, but actively participated.

"A minor cannot consent to any sexual act with an adult.

"Russell, it was *your* responsibility, as an adult and as a parent, to make certain it didn't go there."

"Mr. Bedloe, that's why it was all my fault, not hers. My daughter *participated*, as you put it, because she loves her dad and didn't want to see me in such pain. She did what I asked her to do. She was shocked but did it anyway. I'm her father, for God sake!"

"I know, but I've got a problem with that."

He persists with the subject.

"As a criminal defense attorney, I realize that kids are sexually abused. Anyone who's been in this business as long as I have, has seen what parents can do. But this thing …

"Did you force her to do any of that, or threaten her?"

"*No.* Absolutely not."

"This certainly was not normal behavior between a father and his daughter. You must know that."

Swain is clearly irritated. "Of course I do!"

But Bedloe isn't done.

"Look, I wasn't there but from your descriptions, do you really think she behaved in this manner because, as her father, she did what you *asked* her to do because of your pain? Pain associated with stress? And I don't buy for a second she was under the influence of drugs, not from one five-milligram valium pill.

"Now, you're on the bed, and for whatever the reason or reasons, she changed her mind and told you to stop. But you didn't."

"Mr. Bedloe, it *is* time to stop!"

Despite Swain's emotional reaction, Bedloe asks another question.

"Why did you tell the Isanti County Sheriff's Office and the court that your daughter wanted to continue up to that point?"

Swain answers in frustration.

"Because it was true. Then they turned it around and used it against me, saying it showed callousness and a lack of remorse. That I was lying and trying to blame *her* for what happened. I would not throw my beautiful little girl under a bus like that. I was confused, just trying to answer them. I didn't know what to say, and what not to say. I was scared to death, out of my head. I've never been arrested before. The questions were coming from all directions."

Bedloe continues to confront his client.

"The Alpha Human Services report states that you told them of having sexual thoughts about her before the assault. And, it appears likely she was having such thoughts as well. It would be naïve to think, especially in today's world, that young people her age are incapable of that."

Bedloe wants a response. Swain instead becomes extremely protective.

"Mr. Bedloe, if there's a trial, please, you can't call her. I won't put her through that. She's suffered enough.

*I love her.*"

The lawyer looks deep into his client's eyes, and a very disturbing thought crosses his mind concerning that emotional declaration. He nevertheless goes on without challenging it.

"Russell, I don't need to call her as a witness. Don't be concerned with that. Like I said earlier, it's important to hear it and see it directly from you."

Bedloe smiles.

"What's your daughter's name? On the tattoo. It's hard to read."

"Marcianna. Marcianna Swain."

"How beautiful. It's got a musical rhythm to it."

He motions to the prison guard the meeting is done, and Swain is led back to his cell.


The first week of March, Jeremiah Bedloe calls Lorna, but Victor answers the phone. He is informed that she is undergoing intensive rape psychotherapy with a Lutheran Social Service's psychiatrist at the Gundersen Clinic in La Crosse, and will not be back to work for some time. Victor says that she's doing fine but doesn't want to speak with anyone just yet.


Bedloe gets back to work and spends the next few weeks preparing the post-conviction relief petition, required by the state of Minnesota in order to obtain a trial for his client. He hires a second-year student from Western Technical College's legal secretarial program to type the petition from recorded dictation, rather crude by contemporary standards, but she complies. Once completed on March 24, 2012, he submits it to the Minnesota Court of Appeals, the Minnesota attorney general, the Isanti County court administrator, and the Cambridge city attorney.

Michael Swain stays in Florida until the court's decision is rendered because both agree it doesn't make sense for him to continue researching and contacting potential witnesses for a trial that might not happen.  However, he and Bedloe are in constant telephone contact.

Bedloe keeps the briefcases, and along with other legal cases he has, works steadily on the defense of Russell Swain, all the while hoping that the court will rule in his client's favor. He also calls a number of attorneys he knows personally in the Twin Cities area who have political clout that might help them. He tells them, in so many words, that it's 'payback' time for past favors and legal representation.

The petition is reviewed by the same judge who sent Swain to prison in 2010.  He perfunctorily denies it.  However, on Friday, April 20, 2012, the appellate court overrules the judge. Despite a vehemently heated protest made by that original judge to the appellate court, Bedloe is informed the trial by jury has been granted.

From experience, he knows the prosecution will fight tooth and nail to keep Russell Swain in prison.

By Minnesota law, the trial must be held in the same court the sentencing hearing was held, and neither the prosecution nor the defense can ask for a change of venue.

Further, because the post-conviction relief petition and the two appeals submitted by the public defender's office six months after Russell was sent to prison, stated that the prosecutor and judge in the 2010 sentencing hearing displayed bias and prejudice, Bedloe argues strongly a different prosecutor and judge be assigned to the case. That is granted as well.

When Bedloe hears the news, he immediately calls Michael Swain. The next morning, Michael leaves Florida and drives to La Crosse. Soon thereafter, Russell Swain receives a letter from the state of Minnesota. Everything is set to proceed.

The trial will begin on Monday, June 11, 2012.

The two men spend the next seven weeks going over all the evidence the defense will present. Bedloe subpoenas five in-state witnesses, including three physicians, a forensic psychologist, and a clinical psychologist. In the meantime, Swain receives confirmation from three out-of-state non-subpoenaed witnesses, all experts on 47, XXY-Klinefelter syndrome and the medications prescribed for his son. He then makes travel arrangements for their trip to Minnesota, and room reservations for them.

One week before the start of the trial, Bedloe drives his Corvette to Cambridge, Minnesota, and spends that time selecting jury members.

He and the prosecutor are soon in conflict over the number of jurors. Not surprisingly to either, the prosecution wants six, the defense wants twelve. After considerable discussion, the number is settled at ten.  The jury selection process then begins.

In the end, the jury will consist of six women and four men, ranging in age from twenty-six and sixty-four.  All of them are Caucasian, and three have college or university degrees.

Of the ten jury members, nine have children, and of the nine, two have grandchildren as well.


Bedloe returns to La Crosse on Thursday evening.

# ACT II

## *Scene One*

# The Trial


*On Sunday, June 10, 2012, Jeremiah Bedloe drives a rental car back to Cambridge. Because of the incendiary nature of the crime his client is charged with, for security reason he leaves the Corvette in La Crosse.*

*Michael Swain drove to Cambridge the day before and visited his son in the Isanti County Jail, to which he has been moved for the trial. He's staying at the same motel as Bedloe, but in another room.*

*On Monday morning at 10 a.m., both men take their places in the Minnesota Tenth Judicial District Court, County of Isanti, in the town of Cambridge.*


Bedloe is seated at a table directly in front of the judge's bench. The prosecutor's table is to his left. Directly behind the defense attorney is Michael Swain, sitting on a gallery bench seat in the front row. There are only four other people in attendance.

Russell Swain is led in by a deputy sheriff and sits next to Bedloe, who is immediately angered, for his client is wearing a Department of Corrections prison jumpsuit with his wrists handcuffed and shackles on his ankles.

Michael, angered as well, leans forward and quietly asks: "Jeremiah, why is he in chains and why isn't he wearing the civilian clothes I brought him?"

The attorney needs to stay focused so doesn't take the time to turn and respond. What Swain is not aware of is that the court has the right to have the defendant appear in whatever manner it chooses.

The bailiff announces: "All rise. This Court is in session. The Honorable Loretta H. Guttormsen presiding."

The judge enters the courtroom and sits.

*The woman is tall and slim and close to the same age as Bedloe and Michael Swain. It is quite obvious to everyone that her shoulder length hair is dyed an unnatural dark brown. She wears a copious amount of makeup.*

*Her face is expressionless, with voice a low monotone expressing little emotion. There is an arrogance about her as well, suggesting a courtroom is a monarchy, and she is its queen.*

*Guttormsen's reputation as a hardliner is similar to that of the judge who presided over the sentencing hearing in 2010 – the one that sent Russell Swain to prison.*

*Since Bedloe was not given the opportunity to choose their judge, he feels that the court administration has done so to help assure the same result as the hearing.*

*Bedloe's suspicion to that effect had been confirmed by several area lawyers and he has plans to challenge it soon.*

*The judge starts the trial.*

"Good morning, ladies and gentlemen of the jury. The proceedings we are involved with today, is the case of the State of Minnesota v. Russell Howard Swain. The defendant pleaded guilty to the charge of first degree sexual assault on January 22, 2010 and was sentenced in this court on September 10, 2010, to fifteen years in custody of the Minnesota Department of Corrections with a minimum of nine years to be served.

"The Minnesota Court of Appeals has subsequently ruled, due to new evidence now presented by Mr. Swain's defense counsel, and not known previously, therefore not presented at Mr. Swain's sentencing hearing, along with the accusation of prejudicial conduct by the court during the hearing, that he may therefore withdraw his guilty plea and receive this trial by jury."

She looks at the defendant.

"Mr. Russell Howard Swain, please stand."

Swain and Bedloe stand.

"You sir, have been charged with sexually assaulting a minor, who at the time of the offense, was under the age of thirteen. That is a first degree felony. How do you plead?"

"Not guilty, Your Honor."

"Very well. You may be seated." He and Bedloe both sit.

The judge goes on.

"The prosecutor for Isanti County is Ms. Janet Reese-Hall. Counsel for the defense is Mr. Jeremiah Bedloe. Is the prosecution ready with an opening statement?"

Reese-Hall rises. "I am, Your Honor."


*A woman in her early thirties, the prosecutor is very physically attractive. Her look is complemented by long blond hair, blue eyes, strategically applied makeup, and is wearing a fashionable, colorful dress. All of this suggests she would be a welcomed addition at the nationally televised Fox News Network.*

*Despite a Scandinavian look, Reese-Hall is not a Minnesota native. Married with two children, her family moved here in 2011, previously residing in their hometown of Bloomington, Illinois.*


The prosecutor is about to speak. Bedloe, however, looking for a lull in the proceedings but not finding one, stands.

"Objection." The judge is puzzled and openly annoyed.

"An objection to what? Nothing has been said."

"The defense vehemently protests the court's decision that my client must wear a Department of Corrections monkey suit before this jury. And for heaven sake, can someone kindly remove these chains and shackles.  Mr. Swain has no history of physical violence and is not a threat to flee the country."

"You sir, will sit down now," the judge says without a moment's consideration.  "This court will not tolerate emotional outbursts of any kind.  If you have a complaint concerning the treatment of your client, you will submit it to the court in written form.  Do-you-understand, sir?"

Bedloe sits, and responds.  "Emotional?  I am simply stating a protest."

He looks at the jury.

"In order for my client to receive a fair trial in this court, I will submit the complaint as ruled."

Judge Guttormsen continues.  "Ms. Reese-Hall, proceed."

Reese-Hall walks to face the jury.  She allows time for everyone to recover from Bedloe's outburst.

"Thank you, Your Honor.  Ladies and gentlemen of the jury, please now concentrate on the major fact in this case, namely, that the defendant, Russell Howard Swain, *raped* his minor daughter who was then a girl twelve years of age."

She pauses to scan the jury, allowing them to mentally and emotionally ingest what she just stated.

"There is no other way to describe it.  Actions that led to his behavior were deliberate and planned.  The evidence clearly shows that he *groomed* this little girl for many months, perhaps years, waiting for the opportunity to violate her in a manner no father should be allowed to do."

She turns to face Bedloe.

"The defense will have you believe that there are now substantiated reasons to excuse the defendant's behavior. But let no one be fooled."

The prosecutor then returns to face the jury.

"This innocent little girl, who naturally put total trust in her father, was betrayed to the highest extent imaginable. The defense will attempt to show that genetic, medical, and pharmaceutical reasons were responsible for the defendant's behavior. That ploy is as old as jurisprudence itself."

She then walks slowly and deliberately to face Russell Swain. "The facts in this case are that the defendant knowingly and voluntarily had sexual intercourse with his daughter, a child. Despite her constant pleas he not violate her, the defendant nevertheless maliciously continued until his selfish, immoral desires were met."

The prosecutor looks at each of the ten jurors.

"Those, ladies and gentlemen, are the indisputable facts."

Janet Reese-Hall returns to her table and sits. Judge Guttormsen speaks.

"Mr. Bedloe, your opening statement, please."

Bedloe sits quietly for a moment, and then addresses the jury while remaining seated.

"Consumed by guilt for what he had done on January 2, 2010, Russell Howard Swain emotionally confessed his 'sin' to a man of God, his minister, on January 10, a little over a week later. He did so voluntarily. The minister, not mandated to report his parishioner's confession, took it upon himself to contact the Isanti County Sheriff's Office. My client was arrested that next day, and immediately incarcerated in the county jail."

Bedloe then gets up and walks up to the jury.

"Mr. Swain's confession to his minister, and later to so many others after his arrest, set in motion a chain of events that led him to a prolonged sentence within prison walls.

"What caused him to do this deplorable thing to a girl he dearly loves? Then, why did this highly educated man openly and voluntarily confess his behavior to so many people? He must have known at the time it would certainly destroy everything in his life he worked so hard to achieve. What was he trying to accomplish? Ladies and gentlemen, the answers to these questions are *one* of the reasons why we are here in this courtroom."

He turns to look directly at the prosecutor.

"The defense will not concentrate on what Mr. Swain did, but why he came to do it," then returns to the jury.

"You ten citizens will therefore be asked to focus on the facts presented in this extremely controversial and emotional case. Facts that will thoroughly explain the tragedy that occurred on January 2, 2010."

Bedloe pauses momentarily and then goes on.

"Nothing, I repeat, *nothing* the defense will present will be subjective or hearsay in nature. It will not involve idle opinion nor will it be biased. All of it will be evidence presented by qualified and respected professionals. The evidence will document the physical, mental, and psychological condition Mr. Russell Howard Swain involuntarily found himself in prior to, during, and after that sexual assault, therefore preventing him from making rational decisions."

The defense attorney looks directly at Swain with his voice deeply resonating throughout the courtroom:

"The defense will show, beyond any reasonable doubt, that this good man was unjustly incarcerated in the Isanti County Jail for *eight months* and then unnecessarily sentenced to the Minnesota prison system for *fifteen years.*"

He returns to the jury.

"We are confident that once the facts are presented, you will assist him in achieving the only fair and just alternative to this confinement. *Freedom*, therefore removing his chains and shackles forever."

His statement completed, he goes to the defense table and sits.

Judge Guttormsen says:

"Madam Prosecutor, you may proceed."

## Scene Two

# Witnesses for the Prosecution

"Thank you, Your Honor.  The prosecution calls Ms. Lisa Larsen as its first witness."

Larsen enters the courtroom and walks to the witness stand.  She is then sworn in.

The bailiff asks:

"Do you swear to tell the truth, the whole truth, and nothing but the truth?"

"I do."

"Be seated."


*"Lisa Larsen is very short and stocky, in her late-thirties to early-forties.  She is wearing an Isanti County Sheriff's Office uniform which displays sergeant's stripes.*

*Larsen's hair is jet black and she wears little makeup.  Her voice is normal but quiet, yet she exudes a distinct air of professionalism and occupational toughness.*

*Sitting comfortably in the witness chair, it's clear she's had extensive courtroom experience.*

Prosecutor Janet Reese-Hall begins.

"Good morning, Ms. Larsen."

"Good morning."

"Ms. Larsen, please tell us your professional title."

"I am a special investigator for the Isanti County Sheriff's Office."

"How long have you been with the sheriff's office?"

"I have been with Isanti County for four years. Prior to that, I was a deputy sheriff in Milwaukee County, in Wisconsin, for sixteen years."

"Concerning the State of Minnesota v. Russell Howard Swain, what was your assignment?"

"Once the perpetrator was arrested and incarcerated in the county jail on January 11, 2010, my assignment was to interrogate him."

"How long did your interrogation of the defendant last?"

"Approximately one hour."

"How many times did the two of you meet?"

"Once."

"Did you prepare a report for the Tenth Judicial District Court?"

"Yes."

"Does the folder you are holding contain that report?"

"It does."

"Please relate to the court and the jury what your report states." The prosecutor walks to the witness. Larsen continues.

*"On the morning of January 11, 2010, Isanti County Sheriff's Office Investigator, Chris Lindstrom, received a mandated report concerning Russell Howard Swain, DOB September 12, 1966. Mr. Swain confessed to the reporter that he had sex with his then twelve-year old daughter.*

*"Mr. Swain then proceeded to inform the mandated reporter that he drugged his daughter with the drug diazepam, which he uses for anxiety when flying commercial airlines. He did so by putting a crushed pill in her soft drink.*

*"Later, the defendant confessed to Mr. Lindstrom, that when his daughter started to feel woozy and was slurring her words, the defendant had her sit on his lap. The defendant stated that while rubbing her, he started to get excited. When he finished, he told his daughter he was sorry. The defendant asked her to forgive him, and told her not to tell anyone or he would no longer be able to teach, would lose his license, and go to jail."*

"Then, Officer Larsen, according to your report, you obtained the home address of the victim and her mother in Winona County, Minnesota. You then contacted social services there and they conducted a Corner House interview with this twelve-year old girl. Is that correct?"

"Yes."

The prosecutor then asks what the interview included.

"Well, according to social services there, the girl was visibly upset and crying, stating that she was, in fact, at her father's house on January 2, 2010. She went on to state that she and her dad were sitting in the living room and he was talking to her about having sex with her, and explained how this would enhance their relationship. He then went on to state that they loved each other.

"The girl stated that she said 'no' to her dad several times. Then he put his hand inside her pants and touched the outside of her ... private area. She then stated that she was shocked and confused. She then stated that after the incident, she took a shower and went to bed."

"Investigator Larsen, did you then prepare a search warrant, signed by the Honorable D. Hubert Burger? And what did you find?"

"Yes, it was signed by Judge Burger. During the execution of the search warrant, I found in the defendant's bedroom four sex toys, two of which were vibrators. Also found there were two containers of personal lubricant. I then proceeded to photograph all of the items."

Reese-Hall shakes her head from side to side. "Your Honor, I have no more questions for now."

Judge Guttormsen looks at counsel for the defense.

"Mr. Bedloe, cross-examine?"

"Definitely." He stands and walks to the witness.

"Ms. Larsen, first of all, did your report include that the mandated reporter was a minister?"

"No."

"To my knowledge, you're not an attorney, are you?"

"No, I am not."

"So, you are not aware that, according to Minnesota statutes, ministers cannot divulge the contents of a parishioner's confession without that confessor's permission?"

Reese-Hall objects.

"Your Honor, matters of legal interpretation are not the witness's responsibility. Law enforcement is."

The judge responds, "Objection sustained."

Bedloe angrily retorts: "The witness just put into the record that Russell Swain first confessed to a mandated reporter, his minister. That confession was then subsequently given to Isanti County authorities without my client's permission. That confession, and all subsequent ones as well, are therefore illegally obtained."

"Counsel, the objection is sustained. Move on."

*"Exception."*

"Noted."

Though irritated at the ruling, Bedloe goes on to another subject.

"All right. What about this? Did Winona County prepare a written report of their interview with Mr. Swain's daughter?"

"Written? To my knowledge, no. They recorded it."

"Then how did you find out about what you just testified to?

"A telephone conversation with the counselor."

"Was the counselor male or female?"

Reese-Hall objects while remaining seated, and states: "The counselor's gender is not relevant."

"Sustained," says the judge.

Bedloe presses on and finishes the point.

"From her mouth to your ear. Did the counselor say that intercourse did, in fact, occur?"

"Not in exact words, but she ..."

The prosecutor stands. "Objection. Defense counsel has cleverly included in the record that the counselor was a female, despite the court's ruling its irrelevancy."

"Objection sustained. Counsel's last question will be stricken from the record."

Bedloe looks angrily to the jury. "Ladies and gentlemen, the only person in this entire case who has stated sexual intercourse actually occurred, is Mr. Swain.  Please, keep that in mind."  He returns to the witness.

"Ma'am, in your report, it states that my client bought his daughter a small vibrator and placed it under her mattress.  Yet your search of the residence found sex toys and vibrators in the private domain of the master bedroom, where he and his wife slept.  Nothing was found in the girl's bedroom.  Isn't that correct?"

She hesitates, then answers.  "That is correct."

"Moving on.  Did you find Mr. Swain's computer, and search it for pornography?"

"Yes."

"Did it contain any pornography?"

"Yes."

"Did you find any pornography containing images of children or minors on the computer, in his possession, or anywhere in the house?"

"No."

Bedloe turns and walks toward the jury.  On his way, he goes to his table to pick up the defense's copy of Larsen's report.  His cross-examination is about to become sexually explicit, but he wants to be the one who is forthcoming with the jury.  While facing them, he speaks to the witness.

"Your testimony today did not include *your* interview with the defendant.  When did that interview occur?"

"January 16, 2010."

"In the testimony to the prosecutor a little while ago, you quoted selected portions of Mr. Swain's oral confessions to *others*, but did not include his oral confession to *you*.

"Please read the complete first paragraph on page three of this report, your written version of his *oral confession to you.*"

She starts to read it in silence.

Bedloe looks to the witness, then faces back to the jury. "Aloud, please."

Larsen squirms in her chair, obviously hesitant to comply. Bedloe watches the jury's reaction as she reads:


*"The defendant subsequently disclosed that on the night in question, he and the minor victim were watching a movie together. When the movie ended, the defendant instructed the minor victim to sit on his lap. She did so by straddling her legs over his legs. The defendant said he then told her to stand and remove her pants. She did so and sat again on his lap and they embraced. The defendant instructed the minor victim to again stand and he then removed his shorts, and again had the minor victim sit on his lap. The defendant then again told the minor victim to stand and remove her underpants. After she did so, she again returned to sitting on his lap. The defendant said they sat embracing each other and he became excited and wanted to have sex with the minor victim."*

Bedloe walks back to face the witness.

"I think any objective person would agree that this is a far cry from Winona social services' version of what happened.

"But, be that as it may, as difficult as it was to hear all of what you just read, why is it important for purposes of this trial?

"After your interview with the defendant, your subsequent report consistently states 'he *told* her', 'he *had* her', or 'he *instructed* her' to do the behaviors you listed. However, in Mr. Swain's *written* confessions, which were submitted to Isanti County along with your version of his oral interview, he consistently wrote time after time that 'I *asked* her' to do the behaviors mentioned, all of which she then did.

"Officer Larsen, a comparison of these documents clearly shows a substantial possibility that she may not have been fulfilling his parental *orders* but may have been voluntarily responding to his *requests.*"

Bedloe glares at the witness for some time. Larsen returns the look with an added grin, clearly understanding the lawyer's intent. He waits patiently for the witness, the prosecutor, or the judge, to take the bait.

Reese-Hall obliges.

"Sir, you are *certainly* not implying in a court of law that a rape victim, a minor child, consented. And may I remind learned counsel of the fact that the defendant drugged his daughter."

He responds without looking at her.

"The statutes are very clear concerning consent, and the issue of drugs will be addressed during the defense portion of this trial. The evidence will show it was not a factor."

He immediately goes back to the witness.

"Ms. Larsen, I have two more questions. During your interview with Mr. Swain on January 16, did you note anything peculiar in his behavior, manner of speech, thinking patterns? Anything out of the ordinary."

"No."

"Last question, ma'am. A very important one.

"At the time of his arrest, or shortly thereafter, did the Isanti County Sheriff's Office take blood and urine samples and subsequently have them tested for drugs and alcohol?"

"To my knowledge, no."

"I have completed my questioning of this witness, Your Honor."

"Prosecution, re-direct?"

"No, Your Honor." The judge appears agitated.

"No? Very well. Then call your next witness."

"The prosecution calls Ms. Kimberly Nordquist."

*Employed by the Minnesota Department of Corrections, her role in the case was to interview Russell Swain in the Isanti*

*County Jail and then prepare a report for the sentencing hearing.*

*The interview was conducted six months after Swain's arrest.*

*Bedloe has read the report, and believes it to be extremely biased and opinionated. He was going to subpoena her himself but changed his mind once he saw her name on the prosecution's witness list. He knows Reese-Hall has read the report and she knows that he has done so as well.*

*Kimberly Nordquist is very young, probably no more than twenty-three years of age. She is slim but muscular and is wearing a masculine suit and tie, all of which compliments her deep baritone voice. Her hair is in a short "butch" style and like the previous witness, wears little to no makeup.*

*She enters the courtroom and is sworn in.*


Reese-Hall starts to examine the witness.

"Ms. Nordquist, please state your occupation and place of employment."

"I am a corrections agent for the Minnesota Department of Corrections."

"And what was your role in the Isanti County court sentencing hearing on September 10, 2010?"

"I was assigned to conduct an interview with the defendant, and then prepare a presentence investigation report for the said sentencing hearing."

"How long did the interview last?"

"An hour and thirty-eight minutes."

"Did you then submit that report to the court and appear at the court sentencing hearing on September 10, 2010?"

"I submitted the report to the Isanti County Court on July 14, 2010 but was not called to appear at the sentencing hearing."

"Did you bring that report with you today?"

"Yes, ma'am."

"Please tell the court and the jury what your findings were."

"From the interview, the following was determined.

"First, the defendant's motivation at the time was to receive private sexual offender treatment at Alpha Human Services solely for the purpose of avoiding a prison sentence.

"Second, contrary to the psychosexual evaluation done by a forensic psychologist, suggesting the defendant had but one victim in his past, the Alpha Human Services intake summary indicated several victims.

"Third, the defendant acknowledged he had become aware of his attraction to younger females in 1999 or 2000, and about the year 2007, he heard a commercial on the radio that offered a telephone number to call if the listener was having sexual thoughts about children.  He wrote the number down but never called.

"Fourth, the defendant had an opportunity to address his sexually deviant thoughts but blatantly failed to take the initiative, and as a result, significant harm was done.

"And fifth, he showed no remorse for what he did."

The prosecutor looks at Judge Guttormsen.  "I have no more questions, Your Honor."

Bedloe is looking straight at Reese-Hall, as if to say, "Is that all you have?"

The judge speaks.  "Your witness, counsel."

"Thank you," he says to the judge before standing to address Nordquist."

"Good morning."

She nods to acknowledge the greeting.

Bedloe shakes his head, looking confused at the prosecutor's examination of the woman.  He rubs his chin with thumb and index finger as he walks closer to the corrections agent.

"How long have you worked for the Minnesota DOC?"

"Two years and four months."

Defense counsel responds almost mockingly.

"A long time.  Mr. Swain's pre-sentence investigation report must've been one of your first.

"Are you a college graduate?"

"That is affirmative, I have a bachelor's degree in sociology from the University of Wisconsin at River Falls."

"In assessing the defendant in this case, did you administer any sociological tests?"

"Negative."

"Was there any methodology used to make the determinations you just listed for the court and the jury?"

"Affirmative.  An analysis of his confessions and interviews, along with the sociological research method of naturalistic observation."

Bedloe smiles.

"I remember that one from my college days, many years ago.  I was a double major, psychology and sociology, before law school."

He leans a hand on the witness stand railing, crosses his legs and looks at the ceiling.

"If I recall, 'naturalistic observation' is a research method whereby the sociologist integrates the surroundings being studied, then observes and records the behaviors of people in their natural environment.  Isn't that correct?"

The witness looks intimidated by Bedloe's knowledge.

"Yes sir, that is correct."

"So, you determined what you did by reading the reports submitted by other people, followed by observing Russell Swain for one-and-a half-hours – *after six months in a basement jail cell.*

"Well, madam corrections agent, let's examine what you read and observed."

Bedloe goes to his table and picks up both Alpha Human Services' and Nordquist's reports, along with his glasses. He again rests the reading glasses near the tip of his nose.

"According to the Alpha Human Services report written by Mr. Douglas Wilson, Russell Swain was accepted and ready to receive intense sexual offender treatment that would have lasted two to three years. But *your* report stated he was doing so solely for the purpose of avoiding a prison sentence."

He walks to the agent, shaking her account in front of him.

"Ms. Nordquist, this tidbit of information you included was later utilized by the court in its judgment against my client, to send him to state prison for *fifteen years.* Don't you think he has the right to know how you came to this conclusion?"

He doesn't wait for an answer, but instead holds up the Alpha report.

"How do you know he was manipulating the system for personal benefit, when Mr. Wilson stated just the opposite? In fact, he stated that Mr. Swain was *not* motivated to attend their

123

program in order to avoid prison.  Ma'am, if you're going to use Alpha Human Services' findings, please do so completely and accurately.  And, as we will soon see, this is not an isolated case of your being incomplete and inaccurate."

Bedloe continues to confront Nordquist on another point in her report.


"You then state that Mr. Swain related to Alpha he was having sexual thoughts about young females for some time prior to the assault, and heard on the radio a telephone number to call for help for this reason, but didn't use it.

"In other words, he knew there was a problem in his thinking but didn't know what to do.  Along the way, he got married, with two step-children, was an active church member, has a master's degree, and had a successful teaching position at a St. Paul junior high school.  And, he was then a father to a twelve-year old girl – all at the same time he was having thoughts about children.

*"Thoughts."*

Janet Reese-Hall stands.

"Your Honor, I object.  Is there a question just around the corner the witness will be allowed to respond to?"

"Objection sustained."

Bedloe, however, ignores both women and walks around the courtroom with his arms extended to the side.  Both reports are still in his hands.

"What would I do in that position?  What would most people do?  The moment we told someone of these thoughts, everything we have is lost.  Gone."

Judge Guttormsen insists Bedloe ask a question the witness can respond to.  He aggressively walks back to Nordquist while addressing the court.

"Before I do, it is imperative to this case that a legal differentiation be drawn between thoughts and behavior.  The witness has stated, unequivocally, that the former definitely determined the latter.

"And this also comes on the heels of Isanti County's response that absolutely no child pornography was found on my client's computer or anywhere else in the house.  None." Bedloe pauses, then goes on.  "The prosecutor wants questions the witness can answer?  Okay, here they are.

"Your report goes on to establish that the defendant told Alpha Human Services of three other 'victims' prior to the sexual assault.  Can you elaborate on what transpired during those three occasions?"

The witness responds.  "The defendant stated to Alpha that one of the victims was a thirteen-year old girl and that he fed her alcohol before molesting her."

Bedloe comes back, smiling.  "Ms. Norquist, both were at a party and both were intoxicated at the time.  The defense can call witnesses still residing in La Crosse, Wisconsin, who attended this party and will testify that Russell Swain had nothing to do with her consumption of alcohol. Further, while they kissed, he touched her genitals outside the clothing, however, the witnesses will also testify that she touched his as well.

"Mr. Swain was sixteen at the time, they were both minors. Perhaps you've heard of the 'Romeo and Juliet' stipulation, a misdemeanor? Even if intercourse did occur. Which it didn't. Now, please describe what happened to the next *victim*."

The witness nervously looks at her report. "According to Alpha, on two other occasions, the defendant intoxicated the female victims with alcohol and then molested them."

Bedloe responds, appearing somewhat weary.

"These two victims were, along with Mr. Swain, *adult*s who attended two separate parties on two different occasions, again in La Crosse. In both instances, all were alcohol intoxicated. As in the first case, while kissing, they touched each other's genitals outside their clothing and no intercourse occurred. Witnesses to these events will testify what transpired, stating that the females were *consenting* adults.

"Agent Nordquist, other than his daughter, Mr. Swain has never assaulted anyone, and the Alpha Human Service's report you falsely interpreted, also stated that the defendant had never forced or coerced a female to have sexual intercourse or raped anyone before."

Bedloe suddenly becomes loud and emotional, waving Nordquist's report for all to see.

"In 2010, your document helped give this court the ammunition it needed to make the determination that my client was a sexual predator and should go to prison!"

Bedloe moves away from her, casually walking around in front of the judge's bench, shaking his head while looking at the agent's report. He puts his glasses back on.

"You then stated in your report that, because my client had not addressed his, and I quote, 'sexually deviant thoughts, significant harm has been done,' unquote.

"First of all, I swear, knowing so little of this man, you have nevertheless labeled him manipulative, a serial assaulter, and deviant. Without any doubt, these character appraisals were due entirely to a prejudicial and hair-trigger blind acceptance of his confessions and statements.

"Now, would you please inform the jury how you came to the conclusion that *significant harm* was done to his daughter? Was this naturalistically observed, and if so, how?"

Nordquist responds with anger. "Sir, a girl cannot suffer what that little girl suffered and not be harmed!"

"Oh, so now you're a psychiatrist or psychologist, along with being a sociologist? Let me ask you again, *Doctor* Nordquist, how do you know the girl was harmed? If a corrections agent for the Minnesota Department of Corrections, who is a recent graduate with a bachelor's degree in sociology, states in her report that someone was significantly harmed, but had no concrete professional evidence substantiating that claim, should it have been included at all?"

Bedloe goes to sit, tossing the reports on the table, not interested in any more of the witness's responses. "I won't even bother to discuss the subject of remorse. In fact, your report contains unsubstantiated biased opinions. Nothing more. No further questions."

The judge sternly asks the prosecutor if there is any redirect.

"No, Your Honor."

"Then call your next witness."

Kimberly Nordquist leaves the witness stand. Judge Guttormsen doesn't thank her for appearing. Walking past Reese-Hall, the corrections agent whispers, without looking at her:

"Don't bother calling me again. *Sister."*

The prosecutor ignores the comment and stands. "I call Ms. Kathryn Trussoni."


*Kathryn Trussoni is Russell Swain's first wife and the biological mother of the victim. She and her daughter live in Winona, Minnesota, which is south of Cambridge, and about a three-and a half-hour drive. The woman is rather obese, and just shy of five feet eleven inches tall. For a woman of that size and in her forties, she speaks in a child-like soprano-sounding vocal voice.*

*However, that's where the "child-like" ends.*

*From the beginning, Reese-Hall has regarded Trussoni as her star witness, to clearly illustrate to the jury the truly despicable person that Russell Swain has been.*

*She displayed this same sentiment once before at the court sentencing hearing, when the judge gave her carte blanche to vent her hatred for Swain during the victim impact statement she was allowed to present on her daughter's behalf.*


The witness enters the courtroom, is sworn in, and then sits in the witness chair. Of interest to Bedloe is that she is clutching a significant supply of facial tissue.

Reese-Hall walks to her.

"Ms. Trussoni, you have stated in the past that the relationship between the defendant and his daughter was shrouded in secrecy for a long time. How long?"

"From the age of six."

"And the rape occurred when the girl was twelve. Six years of abuse?"

"Yes. I was divorced from Mr. Swain during that time. My daughter was never allowed to talk about what happened when she was with him during visitations, saying, 'I'm not allowed to talk about anything' and 'I can't talk about that anymore.'"

Bedloe stands and objects.

"This court is again allowing a prosecution witness to give *seriously* biased and unsubstantiated testimony."

"Counsel, your objection is overruled. The witness may answer."

He sits back down, shaking his head while doing so. The prosecutor assists her witness on how to continue.

"And you feel that the sexual abuse of your daughter by Mr. Swain had been ongoing during that entire period?"

Bedloe is again on his feet.

"Objection. "We've heard enough about Mr. Swain's alleged patterns of past behaviors. This trial should be concerned with what occurred on January 2, 2010. Nothing more."

"Counsel, the objection is overruled. The prosecutor's line of questioning is permissible."

"May I ask on what basis the court is allowing the witness to respond to such a sensational line of questioning as this, with absolutely no judicial call for substantiation as to whether or not she is stating facts?"

"The court does not have to answer to you, sir, but to expedite the matter, it is on the basis that you and your client included Ms. Trussoni's victim impact statement in the post-conviction relief petition in order to receive this here trial by jury. The questioning of this witness will continue."

"Your Honor, the witness was mentioned in the petition but was unnamed. Further, nothing she said in the victim impact statement was stated in the petition."

"Mr. Bedloe, the witness will be allowed to answer the prosecutor's questions." She looks to the witness. "Ma'am, you were asked, 'Had the abuse been ongoing for the entire six years.'"

Bedloe is beside himself. The judge is now acting as the prosecutor.

"Yes. And other events that occurred with Mr. Swain my daughter has buried in her mind and may not be known for maybe several years. Her counselor slowly was getting her to the point where she could think about it, or maybe enter some things in a journal about how she feels about everything that happened to her for those many years. Even today, she's embarrassed and ashamed."

The prosecutor emotionally interjects:

"I can only imagine, yet perhaps I cannot."

Bedloe leans back in his chair, looks to the ceiling, and raises his arms in complete frustration. "You can't be serious. This is a court of law, not Cambridge neighborhood gossip!"

Judge Guttormsen states: "Sidebar."

Bedloe and Reese-Hall walk to the side of the courtroom where Judge Guttormsen stands waiting.

"Mr. Bedloe, this court will determine what is and what is not acceptable. And, the prosecutor will be allowed to present her case as I determine. Is that clear? Also, stop with the snide comments. They have no place in a court of law."

She turns to face the prosecutor.

"Madam Prosecutor, you will refrain from adding your personal opinions for the jury to hear."

They all return to their respective stations. Bedloe has just started his psychological warfare with the prosecutor and the court. Judge Guttormsen bangs her gavel down and speaks to the courtroom.

"Ladies and gentlemen, it is almost noon. We are adjourned until one-thirty."

"All rise," says the bailiff.


Bedloe and Michael Swain are walking to the attorney's rental car to find somewhere to have lunch, when Bedloe notices a small piece of paper folded several times jammed in the driver's side door. He pulls it out, unfolds it, and reads:

*'medical center owns someone on the court'*

They get in the car and he gives it to Swain. They both look at each other. Swain speaks first.

"Who do you think wrote it?"

"I have no idea. Also, how did someone know this is my car?" He scans the area. "For some reason, I'm being watched."

They drive along slowly, when Bedloe abruptly heads back to their motel.

"I'm skipping lunch, have to make a phone call."

"Here, use my cell."

"No. I'll use the phone in my room. Take your truck and get something to eat. I'll meet you back in the courtroom."

Bedloe sits on the motel bed and looks up a telephone number in his small pocket address book. He calls Toby Tollefson, a private investigator in St. Paul that he's used in the past. He tells Tollefson to find any connections between the MidState Medical Center and the Isanti County Court. The P.I. says he'll get on it right away.

*Monday afternoon, one-thirty p.m. Prosecutor Reese-Hall continues with her witness.*

"Ms. Trussoni, just before the recess this morning, you were talking about your daughter's journal and her feelings about the ongoing abuse. Do you feel that irreparable harm has been done?"

"Certainly. It's obvious her relationships with the opposite sex will always be affected by all those encounters. And, my daughter will always have trouble with anyone in authority since Mr. Swain held that position. Her relationship with Mr. Swain is a basic fundamental relationship in which you base all others in life. It would be impossible."

Bedloe stands. "Objection, testimony based on conjecture."

"Overruled."

As if on cue, Trussoni starts to cry. Bedloe continues the objection.

"Your Honor, as defense stated this morning, the witness is giving an unsubstantiated 'lecture.' These are merely her biased opinions, not based on substantiated facts."

"Counsel, your objection is overruled."

Defense counsel continues to stand, now with clenched fists on his hips and shaking his head. The prosecutor moves on.

"Ms. Trussoni, this morning we were discussing the personal interactions between your former husband and his daughter, especially from six years of age until she was raped at age twelve. During this entire period of time, do you believe Mr. Swain sexually desired your daughter?"

"Of course, but I don't believe for a second that his obsessive deviant behavior was limited to only my daughter. It started long, long before that. Probably even before I knew him."

"Not only with your daughter, but with others as well?"

"Yes."

"Can you give the jury examples?"

"I certainly can."

Jeremiah Bedloe again challenges the judge.

"This trial concerns the January 2, 2010 sexual assault. To allow this witness' so-called interpretations of my client's alleged patterns of past behaviors – as other witnesses have also done in this trial, is irresponsible for purposes related to these judicial proceedings."

The judge responds. "I overruled the objection then and now. However, madam prosecutor, please keep your questions relevant to the trial's purpose."

"I will, Your Honor."

Bedloe sits. The prosecutor smiles smugly and throws defense counsel's objection back in his face.

"Ms. Trussoni, the question had to do with patterns of behavior you have witnessed."

"Yes, ma'am. Mr. Swain and I were divorced in 2003 but both continued working for the legal analyst at Winona State University. One day she called me aside, the legal analyst, and said that she saw Mr. Swain viewing pornography on the internet and that I should be very cautious about letting my daughter be around him."

The witness continues matter-of-factly.

"Also, his employment record at other schools before that time included many firings for sexual harassment and viewing pornography on the internet while working."

"Did you inform anyone about these behaviors?"

Bedloe stands. "Objection. What this witness just testified to is about as slanderous as it gets. The defense demands the names of every person and school she just referred to, so they can be contacted to verify these horrendous charges."

Judge Guttormsen outright ignores Bedloe's demand, telling the witness to answer the prosecutor's question. Defense counsel is stunned to the extent it renders him speechless.

"I presented it all to the Winona County Court but somehow they still found it necessary to continue his seeing my daughter. Unfortunately, the legal system thought it best over the years to actually *increase* his time with her and not decrease it. It was so unbelievable."

Reese-Hall moves on to another subject. "Let's go back to the day of the rape itself if you don't mind. The defendant admitted to placing a sedative medication in your daughter's soft drink, unbeknownst to her. Is that correct?"

Trussoni's face becomes disturbingly explosive, her voice piercingly shrill. She looks directly at Russell Swain. "Yes. And I would also like the jury to fully think about what that man used on my daughter to selfishly get what he wanted."

Crying and dabbing her lower eyelids with tissue, she points directly to Swain. "Those drugs were intended for *you,* with a dosage of the appropriate concentrated amount for someone such as yourself, who was at that time, three times my daughter's weight. You could've *killed* her with that drug. You drugged an innocent twelve-year old, and in a heartbeat took her bright future away from her. You deserve to die in prison!"

Bedloe is half-way to his feet to object, especially for the potential "killer" comment and her wish Swain would die in prison. However, the attorney stops short for one reason. He's been studying this woman, mentally dissecting every part of her testimony, trying to determine the reason or reasons behind her intense hatred and motivation to completely destroy her former husband. He slowly sits down, silent.

Trussoni leans forward in the witness chair and buries her face in tissue, sobbing uncontrollably. Bedloe could've easily objected to the witness speaking directly to his client but allows that to go by as well.

The prosecutor continues, and strategically hits the defense attorney right between the eyes with a subject he is totally unaware of and unprepared for.

And that is something Jeremiah Bedloe will not tolerate. Reese-Hall continues:

"Your daughter wrote a letter to the judge who presided over the sentencing hearing. Did you bring that letter with you?" The witness nods. "Would you mind reading it?"

"I'll try, but I must leave out her first name."

*'Dear Judge. My name is 'blank' Swain. I do not want to testify. I am very disappointed in my father's actions. I trusted*

*him. I don't want to see him again. It would be very challenging for me to see him. He has betrayed me and I will never forget or forgive him for that.'"*

Bedloe slowly rises, his face red with anger.

"All right. This has now gone *far enough.* Your Honor, is this letter a matter of record and therefore allowed to be examined by the defense?"

"It's 'yes' to both matters, sir."

Bedloe looks fiercely at the prosecutor.

"Today is the first I've ever heard of this letter. Did the girl sign it?"

Reese-Hall responds without looking at him.

"She did."

Defense counsel goes back to the judge, and says:

"Due to Russell Swain's wishes, defense attorneys have not included his daughter's appearance at the sentencing hearing or at this trial. However, now that she is a part of the trial, by indirect testimony, I suspect that the letter just read was *not* authored by a then twelve-year-old girl."

Bedloe walks to the middle of the courtroom, half-way between the judge and the prosecutor, looking at them both while speaking. He aggressively points directly to the witness.

"I would suggest to the court that the letter was authored by Ms. Trussoni, by telling the girl what to write and then telling her to sign it. Therefore, it is crucial to my client's case that his daughter now sign a sworn and witnessed affidavit, stating these are her own words and not those of the witness. And this affidavit should then be presented to the court forthwith."

He returns to his table, but stops and again faces the judge.

"Or, if the court prefers, bring Mr. Swain's daughter to Isanti County to state under oath, and not in the presence of her mother, that the letter was written by her and *only* her."

Judge Guttormsen looks nervously at Reese-Hall as Bedloe sits, angrily awaiting the court's decision.

"Do you have any objection to these requests?"

Bedloe quickly challenges the bench.

"Your Honor, this is *your* decision and no one else's."

The judge uncharacteristically yells:

"Counsel, I will decide whose decision it is! Ms. Reese-Hall?"

"Yes, Your Honor, I object. Ms. Trussoni is under oath in this courtroom, so the question as to the letter's authorship should be addressed to the witness."

The judge is momentarily silent, then gives her decision. "I agree. Ma'am, you are under oath. Did your daughter, in fact, write this letter on her own?"

Trussoni spontaneously turns, facing the jury, to the left of Judge Guttormsen.

"Of course, Your Honor. She wrote it with no help from me. They're her words."

The judge looks down at her bench littered with papers, moves a few pieces around, and then states her ruling.

"The defense's objection is overruled. Continue, Madam Prosecutor."

Bedloe taps his fingers on the table all the while in thought, and then stands in defiance.

"Your Honor, I wish to address this Tenth Judicial District Court."

The judge responds sharply, almost defensively.

"What now, counsel? Yes, yes, address the court if you must."

In his commanding voice, Bedloe bellows a stern conclusion designed for everyone in the state of Minnesota to hear.

"Today, and by history in 2010, this district court has continued to allow biased and prejudicial unsupported testimony, including its stance to reject and overrule all objections I have made on this issue.

"I see no indication that the court will abandon this blatant sexism, making it *impossible* for me to continue with an objective defense of my male client.

"Therefore, I request permission to withdraw from the case."

The now increasingly populated courtroom becomes very turbulent. Janet Reese-Hall stands and nearly shouts: *"Sexism?"*

Bedloe glares at her, nodding. "It cuts both ways, missy."

Russell Swain jumps to his feet.

"Mr. Bedloe. Please, you can't leave me!"

His father also stands, tightly gripping the bannister in front of him.

Bedloe starts packing papers back into the briefcases and responds to his client.

"*Why not?* This whole God-forsaken case is clearly stacked against you – and me."

He looks at Reese-Hall and Judge Guttormsen, then waves his arms at the entire courtroom proceedings – including the female prosecution witnesses:

"There's been enough estrogen in this courtroom to float the Royal Norwegian Navy. Hell, they might just as well find the nearest oak tree in this town and *hang you, or maybe castration would be preferable. Or both.*"

Judge Guttormsen is now on her feet as well.

*"You sir, are in contempt of this court."*

Bedloe walks to her bench and snaps back.

"You have no idea how much contempt I have for this court."

"Mr. Bedloe, you are hereby fined ten thousand dollars or ordered to serve six months in jail."

Bedloe reaches into his sport coat vest pocket.

"I will post bond right here and now. Who should the check be made out to? *You?*"

Judge Guttormsen responds in obvious anger.

"What is meant by *that?* Never mind. This court is in recess. The jury will remain seated until the bailiff tells you to leave. Ms. Reese-Hall and Mr. Bedloe, join me in my chambers. *Now."*


In her chambers, the judge walks to a small refrigerator and extracts a can of soda, then goes to sit in her oversized leather chair, trying all the while to calm herself.

"Sit down. Both of you, sit down."

The defense attorney and prosecutor sit facing the judge, who continues while nervously drinking.

"Well, this one takes the cake, by golly. I've been on the bench for almost eighteen years now."

She looks at Bedloe and smiles, slowly nodding her head. "You're a doozy, Jerry. A real hand full."

Bedloe cringes at the name, simultaneously noting a change of personality in the woman with the black robe.

The judge then looks at Reese-Hall. "And you, Jan, I must say, you're standing right up there with him."

Guttormsen gives out with a loud and boisterous laugh, which Bedloe knows is bogus and clearly for the purpose of disguising her nervousness. She then shakes her head while looking out the office window, suddenly appearing worried.

"I have never seen a case like this, or the town in such a dither about a trial before. The media, the T.V. people are starting to come and mill around in the courtroom and outside there. News travels fast in these parts, you know." The judge then turns back to the two with a sympathetic smile.

"Look, I realize this kind of case can make tempers short, so I'm trying to understand the pressures you two are under and help … be fair with you here."

Both attorneys are dumbfounded by these sudden frivolous attempts at cordiality, all preposterously counterfeit.

Bedloe smiles. "Judge Guttormsen – Lorie – the only pressure I feel is coming from the bench, and your rulings."

The judge frowns uncomfortably at the disrespectfully abbreviated first name, but quickly tries to keep the informality going. "Now, come on now, don't be so paranoid, for gosh sakes."

Bedloe gets up and walks to a window. He spots a lone bird flying in the open blue sky and for a moment, envies the creature.

He puts his hands in the corduroy sport coat's outer hip pockets and turns while looking to the floor, shaking his head all the while. He speaks to the judge in a moderate, rational tone, simultaneously studying a mental map he's drawn in the case.

"A transcript of the trial up to this point would definitely substantiate the number of objections I have made that were overruled. Then, the ones the prosecutor's made that were sustained. The comparison would show how fair you've been, and how paranoid I am. And, if by some small miracle I continue in this trial, that practice must change!"

The defense attorney sits back down. Prosecutor Reese-Hall speaks.

"Your Honor, perhaps counsel should be reminded of the fact that the court and prosecutor's office has accepted every one of his defense witnesses without question or debate."

The judge smiles at Bedloe.

"Jan has a point there."

Bedloe counters while looking at the prosecutor.

"That is due to their credibility, not the generosity of this county."

Again he stands and continues while walking back and forth.

"Since the day Isanti County sent Russell to prison two years ago, his father has worked harder than any parent on earth to find reasons why his son did what he did to his granddaughter.

"As his son's designated power of attorney, once all of what he found in the vast number of records and reports he's reviewed is presented to this court by the defense, certain people around here could very well lose professional reputations and millions of dollars in civil damages. You know it, and I know it."

He walks to the ornate table near the judge's desk filled with family portraits and pictures of state officials and other noteworthy individuals. He turns to face the two women.

"Let me be even *more* frank. These influential people have already been told who our witnesses are and what they'll be testifying about. I have some idea how that happened.

"They now know what we've got, are getting very nervous, and have to find any way they can to cover their asses."

He looks at both Guttormsen and Reese-Hall as he goes on.

"You want to hear paranoia? Okay, here it is. I think someone involved in this trial is assisting them in order to assure a guilty verdict, therefore sending my client back to prison and eliminating any possible law suits. That will happen only over my dead body!"

Judge Guttormsen and prosecutor Reese-Hall look stunned first at each other, then to Bedloe. The judge's contrived cordiality is gone, and she now conveniently gazes at the prosecutor. She then returns to Bedloe.

"Counsel, are you suggesting that a conflict of interest has penetrated this court and this trial?"

"No, ma'am. What may be penetrating this court is *malfeasance."*

The judge stands and challenges him.

"Malfeasance? How? Who?"

"I don't know yet but I'm getting there."

"Then how did you come by this knowledge?"

"Some anonymous person left a note on my car."

"A note? An anonymous note left on your car, that's it? Show it to me."

Bedloe responds loudly, in essence stating the note is not available.

"I ate it."

The judge asks a nervous question of the prosecutor, a readily available scapegoat.

"Do you have any knowledge of this matter?"

Reese-Hall becomes quite upset at the mention of it and angrily responds to the judge.

"Your *Hon*or."

Guttormsen's eyes are now searching Bedloe's face, sensing a ploy is in the making to get one of them to slip up and concede something.

"Wait a minute here. Does this have anything to do with the court's rulings on your objections? If that's the case, you don't want to bark up that tree, mister. It will not deter me from conducting this trial any differently."

The judge sits back down. Bedloe watches and listens closely as she goes on.

"Besides, you know as well as I do, malfeasance is historically extremely difficult to substantiate, along with intent and knowledge. I would suggest you confine your efforts to this trial and *only* this trial, and not go off chasing some hare-brained conspiracy theories you're concocting."

The judge goes to open the door to her chambers and calls for the bailiff.

"Inform the jury that the trial will reconvene tomorrow morning at nine."

Guttormsen then addresses the prosecutor.

"You will resume your examination of Kathryn Trussoni at that time. I want this trial over and done with by the end of the week."

She turns to face Bedloe.

"What about you? In order to get this trial over with, I'll drop the contempt charge."

Bedloe nods, then leaves the judge's chambers and walks toward the Isanti County Jail. The sharp sound of high heels clacking on the sidewalk behind him makes him stop. He looks back to see the prosecutor running after him.

She stoutly faces him.

"Damn it, man, how certain are you about this?"

They both scan the area to see if anyone's watching.

"I've suspected something even before the trial began but wasn't able to put my finger on it.  Then I got the note."

"Could it be jury tampering?"

"No."  He doesn't offer any more.

Reese-Hall shakes her head in sudden worry and disgust, then barks:

"I'll see you in court tomorrow."

She starts to leave, then Bedloe asks her a question.

"Why did you call Nordquist to the stand?  You read her report, yet served her up to me on a silver platter."

Realizing his cross-examination of her first two witnesses was "textbook," and also aware of her own insecure feelings concerning Trussoni's emotional state and reliability as a witness, she walks back to the older veteran attorney.  With a defensive sneer, she whispers loudly:

"Just do your goddamned job, and I'll do mine!  Okay?" Then she walks away.

Bedloe goes to the Isanti County Jail and asks for permission to see Russell Swain.  They meet with a concrete block wall and a 12-inch by 12-inch plexiglass window separating them, and speak using intercom telephones.  He informs Swain of his decision to continue in the trial. His client starts to cry with relief. Bedloe does not mention the note or the conversations with the judge and the prosecutor.

Once through with Swain, he asks a jail employee if there's a public pay phone in the building. The man nods and points down the hall. Bedloe finds it and reaches into his sport coat inner pocket for the small phone book, then dials Toby Tollefson's number. An automated operator states the charge and Bedloe puts in the necessary coins.

He gets Tollefson's answering machine and leaves a message.

"Toby. Bedloe. It's the judge. Loretta H. Guttormsen, G-u-double t-o-r-m-s-e-n. Find out what you can about any possible connections between her and the medical center. Call me back at my motel when you come up with something. I may or may not need it but I want to be ready. Talk to you soon."


*Tuesday morning, nine a.m. Kathryn Trussoni has returned to the witness stand. Before the trial continues, Judge Guttormsen addresses the jury.*


"The court wishes to apologize for the unfortunate scene you witnessed yesterday. All parties met in my chambers and we discussed the future of this trial. Due to the rational atmosphere that prevailed during that meeting, this court has dropped contempt charges against defense counsel and he has graciously consented to continue representing his client.

"Ms. Reese-Hall, you may continue."

"Thank you, Your Honor.  She walks to the witness.

"Ms. Trussoni, the defense is claiming that an illness was in some way responsible for the defendant's behavior with your daughter.  It's referred to as *Klinefelter syndrome*.  He was born with this thing."

Reese-Hall glances at Bedloe while addressing the witness.

"Defense counsel will produce several witnesses who will testify that this illness can cause numerous psychological disorders.  Having known the defendant, and having once been married to him for some years, do you recall him being treated for anything having to do with that?"

Trussoni's face is clearly expressing to the jury that Russell Swain is faking.

"*No.*  Please, I beg you to be careful with this.  He's still desperate for the court to think that only one extra chromosome, the Klinefelter syndrome in some of his cells, is to blame."

She leans forward and tightly grips the railing enclosing the witness stand, dramatically nodding her head.

"He … he also said that what he did was due to sleep deprivation or depression of some kind.  But I know better.  What he did to my daughter was something planned out over a long period of time.

"This crime did *not* occur due to lack of sleep, depression, or anything else. He *groomed* my beautiful daughter for several years, waiting for the opportunity to take her innocence away for his own selfish, pathetic needs."

Trussoni is again sobbing heavily. Bedloe is aware the witness knows she has everyone's attention, but also senses she is possibly close to stumbling in some way. He lets the questioning continue without objecting.

"Ms. Trussoni, as previously mentioned, you lived with Russell Swain for six years, and knew him intimately for quite a few years prior to that. As a former friend and spouse, why are you so concerned that he might potentially be released from prison?"

"I've known Mr. Swain for almost twenty years. That's how long. He's a habitual liar and a good showman. He's avoided every potentially bad situation he's gotten himself into by being deceptive and manipulative. It may appear he's amenable to probation and treatment, but it's just another scam. I fear that he's got all these people here believing he's ..."

She pauses and again looks to the jury, speaking very rapidly and gasping for breath with each deeply emotional plea.

"Please, if he can get you to believe all this, he will be free to roam and victimize other children. I don't believe for a *second*, when you consider his prior actions, he'll be able to stay away from my daughter unless he is in prison."

Bedloe looks down at his relaxed, interlaced hands. He has just been presented with the reason for this woman's intense hatred for Russell Howard Swain.

The witness for the prosecution continues her Gatling-gun delivery, the volume of her voice increasing as she continues.

"My daughter and I spoke about all this at bedtime after the arrest. She wanted to stay updated on the events of the case, and with her counselor's permission, I did that.

"When I read the motion for dispositional departure to my daughter, a very scared look came over her face and her words to me were, 'He didn't seem depressed or sleep deprived to me.' That was as far as we discussed this motion because after uttering those words, she cried for a good half-hour."

Responses are rehearsed and memorized, the words exiting her mouth in continued rapid-fire with eyes becoming wider. Reese-Hall clearly sees the changes in her witness too.

"Ms. Trussoni, try to relax. I know this is difficult for you. Throughout this entire ordeal that you and your daughter have suffered, have you ever seen remorse on the part of the defendant?"

"None. There's no remorse in that … *person*, even today. Anyone could tell. My mother and father were with me at the hearings prior to the sentencing hearing, and none of us saw a shred of remorse.  And if there *was*, believe me, it was not genuine."

She looks directly at the jury.

"Everything Mr. Swain says or does is a total pack of lies, and only for one purpose – to selfishly get what he wants!"

As Trussoni continues talking, she notices that most of the jury members are now concentrating on Russell Swain.  In a flash, her face suddenly becomes melodramatically fearful with body upright and erect while sitting, courageously challenging her former husband in a theatrical manner.

The woman wants center stage all to herself.  Bedloe objects to none of it.

Then, Trussoni portrays Swain as a threat to society.


"If he's released to a non-secure treatment facility like he's trying for here again, I and my entire family will not be able to remain in our homes.  The fear is that great.  We would need to move and essentially go into hiding in a different city, perhaps even a different state."

"He is a *predator* and knows where we live.  He knows our habits and could easily prey on a member or members of our family again.  My mother is especially afraid of Mr. Swain.  She fears for her life if he's freed."

Her eyes are now wild with anxiety. Bedloe doesn't even challenge the "predator" characterization for now. There's time for that later on, he figures.

Trussoni goes on.

"But especially children, my God, he could be free to prey on the most vulnerable population. The little ones."

She looks wide-eyed at the jury with her mouth gaping open, but suddenly decides not to speak any further. The courtroom is nervously still.

The prosecutor feels she should say something to finalize the witness's emotional statements. Everyone, including Bedloe, stares at Trussoni as Reese-Hall proceeds.

"Your Honor, we have no more questions, subject to redirect. However, I would like to say just one more thing if allowed."

"Yes, go ahead."

She walks to stand directly in front of the defendant and reads from a piece of paper she is holding. There is little emotion in her voice.

"At the conclusion of the court sentencing hearing in 2010, *that* prosecutor stated, referring to Russell Howard Swain:


'Through this man's selfish actions, he's murdered the person this little girl could have been and would have been.'"

She then goes to the jury.

"Ladies and gentlemen, the sole reason why we are here is to best serve the needs of this precious child, by providing the facts in this sad case. Your witness, Mr. Bedloe."

The prosecutor returns to her seat.

Russell Swain looks at Bedloe with a really worried expression. It appears to him as though his lawyer didn't challenge enough the flagrantly harmful testimony from Kathryn Trussoni.

However, Bedloe knows this strategy to let her continue talking uninterrupted will eventually work in his client's favor.

The judge speaks.

"Counsel, cross-examine."

Bedloe swings his chair to directly face Reese-Hall.

She counters with a confident smile, one that indicates she can taste victory.

## Scene Three

# Hell Hath No Fury

Slowly getting up, Jeremiah Bedloe continues to look long and hard at Janet Reese-Hall.

The defense attorney turns to face the gallery, and his eyes focus to Michael Swain who, like his son, appears worried.

He glances toward the rear of the now packed courtroom, and to his astonishment, sees Lorna Dunn and her husband, Victor. They are standing against the back wall. Bedloe and his secretary smile warmly to one another, and he immediately notes a dramatic change in her appearance.

The judge repeats:

"Counsel, cross-examination."

Bedloe struggles to regain focus on the tasks at hand. He returns to face the front of the courtroom and concentrates on the many areas of cross-examination he must cover, searching for the best starting point. After so many years, he knows it'll come to him.

He reaches down and pats his client's shoulder, then walks to the jury with hands clasped behind him. Bowing his head while going, he shakes it from side to side, smiling. This gesture, after such an emotional display by the prosecution's witness, is perhaps not the wisest thing to do. However, a definite mood needs to be set in the courtroom, one that prefaces what is to come.

Bedloe grips the jury box railing and begins softly, but he will soon build the cross-examination to a crescendo.

"Ladies and gentlemen, a Minnesota defense attorney cannot state an objection during a victim impact statement. Therefore, when Kathryn Trussoni gave *that* statement for her daughter in 2010, my client's attorney at the time was required to remain mute.

"However, *this is now a trial by jury*."

With his penetrating eyes and fiercely intimidating "game face" glower, he turns to look straight at the witness for the prosecution.

"And you ma'am, are subject to cross-examination concerning what was stated then and now. So, let's begin."

Bedloe walks back to his table to retrieve a legal pad. He reaches for the reading glasses and puts them on, ready for business.

"Ms. Trussoni, it has been stated by you over and over again, that Mr. Swain's relationship with his daughter was, and I quote, 'shrouded in secrecy and that sexual abuse had been ongoing since the age of six' – unquote."

He looks combatively at Trussoni.

"What evidence or statements do you have from your daughter that confirms that allegation?"

She snaps back with indignation, immediately standing up to her adversary.

"I don't need *statements* from my daughter. I'm her mother, so I *knew* it was going on."

"How? Was it something you sensed in her? Did you see it yourself? Was there a dramatic change in mood or personality? Eating habits? Physical evidence? Did a pediatrician examine her and find evidence of any kind? Bruises, cuts, abrasions? Signs of a struggle? *Anything.*"

She doesn't respond but smiles smugly, confident the courtroom and its occupants are clearly on her side. Bedloe joins in with a similar facial expression.

"Very well, silence is golden, or so it's said.

"Next, please provide this jury with objective evidence of continuous, if any, *grooming* of her by your then husband.

"Did she tell you Mr. Swain did or said anything to her since the age of six? I assume your daughter is able to speak."

Trussoni responds quite impatiently.

"As I stated before sir, she wouldn't talk about it. When I asked how her visit was with her fath ..., Mr. Swain, she always became withdrawn and wouldn't answer."

"You can say it, ma'am, she has a father."

Trussoni sneers. "She does, but it's not him."

Bedloe turns to face the jury, shaking his head at her self-consumed "dagger" comment. Reese-Hall rolls her eyes,

159

indicating that the remark was counterproductive and meant to hurt. A few people on the jury look to each other and seem to question the meaning behind the witness' remark. Bedloe addresses all of the ten jurors.

"By that statement, the witness refers to the fact that Russell Swain is not the girl's biological father. This will be fully explained during the defense portion of the trial."

Bedloe moves on.

"Returning to grooming. As many of us are aware, the term refers to the psychological manipulation of a child in various ways, and is entirely for an ulterior motive.

"For example, this is done by expressing affection for the child, gaining their trust, positively reinforcing the child, participating in activities with the child, and so on. While normal parents do these things out of love, the predator, however, does them to prepare the victim for sexual reasons."

He walks back to the witness.

"Specifically, Ms. Trussoni, what examples of these manipulations, or others for that matter, were evident in my client that led you to state he was grooming his daughter for that reason?"

"All of them."

"How do you know they were done for sexual reasons and not simply due to his devotion to her?"

"A devoted father would not do what that man did to his daughter!"

"Ma'am, your response, as damaging as you intended it to be, does not, in any way, substantiate that his motivation was for sexual reasons.

"Do you have evidence that Mr. Swain ever exposed your daughter to pornography for the purpose of eventually normalizing sexual behaviors in her mind?"

"No, I do not."

"Do you have evidence that he talked to her continuously, if at all, about explicit sexual matters?"

"No."

Bedloe goes and faces his client while continuing with the witness.

"Ms. Trussoni, your claims that Mr. Swain abused and groomed his daughter for years were previously taken as *fact*, but the day has come that you are now required to substantiate all the accusations presented at the sentencing hearing and here today.

"If you do not prove or recant those statements, a law suit could be filed against you for slandering and defaming this man's character. Do you understand that?"

She responds loudly, getting back on track and continuing her demeaning description of the defendant.

"'Character?' What character?"

The prosecutor objects. Defense counsel turns to her.

"Your Honor, the defense is threatening and badgering the prosecution's witness." Bedloe responds.

"And I object to this witness' unrelenting disparaging comments concerning …"

Trussoni stares at the jury and loudly overpowers Bedloe before he has time to finish.

"He abused and groomed her. I'm her mother. For the love of God, I would know. Wouldn't I? They are *not* accusations. They are *facts.*"

Bedloe hits his open hand hard against the witness stand railing.

"Then give us *proof* of these facts. *Ma'am, this is a court of law.* So far, all that has been heard here are your opinions."

He continues.

"In case you are not familiar with the meaning of the word fact, let me give you a definitive example.

"Official court statements and reports by two psychologists, with decades of professional experience specializing in victim and sexual offender treatment, both stated shortly after my client's arrest, that there was absolutely *no history* of his either abusing or grooming his daughter. *None.*"

Trussoni looks again at the jury and responds, her arms outstretched.

"Who, what are they? Strangers. I'm her *mother.*"

Bedloe also looks to the jury and in an effort to rebut her repetitious comment, nods his head repeatedly and states:

"I know, I know, you're her mother. Then, I repeat. As her mother, give this jury evidence. Are we merely to take your word for everything because of your maternal status?"

In a battle for the truth, he returns to the witness and expands on the superfluous theme.

"Use your daughter's school counselor's reports if you have them, or statements from family members ... doctors."

Bedloe throws his arms to the ceiling, sharply stating:

*"Or have her write another letter to the judge."*

He turns away from her momentarily.

The eyes of the witness are now scarlet with rage and defiance, as she no doubt perceives Bedloe's outburst as the assault on her credibility that it was. But then she smiles with spite, clearly attempting to annoy the enemy.

Bedloe turns and sees her facial expression and aggressively challenges her with his perceived self-evident truth.

"In fact, Ms. Trussoni, there *was* no abuse. And what you characterized was grooming was, in fact, her father expressing care and love."

At this declaration, her emotions become snarled and a ricocheting bullet. She no longer attempts to hide the rage with her counterfeit smile.

"Care and love?  That's ridiculous.  *God damn it, he killed my daughter's future, my beautiful daughter.*  You call that care and love?"

Judge Guttormsen picks up her gavel, about to criticize the witness' language.  The prosecutor stands and pleads with Bedloe, implying he should move on to another subject.

"Mr. Bedloe, please.  The woman is under tremendous stress."

Bedloe still looks at Trussoni but responds to the prosecutor.  The intensity of his defense is escalating.

"This witness's stress is a walk in the park on a sunny day, Madam Prosecutor, in comparison to my client staring in the face of close to *five thousand more sunrises behind bars.*"

He goes to the table for his legal pad and reading glasses, returns to the witness, and goes on to another subject.


"Ms. Trussoni, you stated that what Mr. Swain did to his daughter will, and I quote, 'psychologically affect her to the extent that it will cause future problems with the opposite sex and with all authority figures for years to come' – unquote.  Is that correct?"

"It is common sense, it will."

He takes off his glasses and holds them in his hand.

"Are you a psychologist or a psychiatrist?"

"Of course not."

"Has your daughter ever been under the care of either?"

The witness responds with great impatience. "No-no-no. She sees a school counselor."

"Is this *counselor* trained in sexual abuse therapy? Does he or she have a master's or doctorate in school psychology and received training in treating such matters?"

"I don't know. I don't know."

Bedloe shakes his head.

"It appears this case is filled with experts who are not experts. Yet, you are absolutely convinced your daughter's future is destroyed by what occurred on January 2, 2010."

"*Yes.* I am absolutely certain. It's very obvious."

Bedloe looks at the jury members while dropping the legal pad on his table. He then walks around the courtroom, scanning all the people present, and then returns to address the witness softly and calmly.

"Ms. Trussoni, in today's world, parents and teachers can attest to the torturous pain sexually abused children suffer. And we are all being educated to know what to look for, signs these abused children exhibit in behavior, such as negative changes in mood, sociability, and lacking trust in adults, for example, that would signal something is dreadfully wrong.

"However, in objectively examining your daughter's future, it is imperative to state the distinct possibility that this may not be the case. The reasons could be many."

He goes to the jury and addresses them while grabbing hold of the railing surrounding the jury box. He understands that what he is about to say could be misinterpreted, yet takes the risk and proceeds.

"It's commonly known that Russell Swain's daughter greatly enjoyed communicating on a regular basis with members of her extended family, including her father's. She routinely sent birthday and seasonal cards, as well as short letters with pictures of herself in various social situations.

"Members of Mr. Swain's family are prepared to testify that right after the sexual assault, and surprisingly to them, there was no drop off concerning these communications. They did start to taper off shortly after her father's arrest.

"Before they eventually stopped being sent, the letters and pictures vividly depicted her continuing participation in team sports and school activities, *all* in the company of peers and with adult supervision – many of whom were men. In one picture, she had an arm comfortably draped around the shoulder of her male soccer coach, smiling happily.

"Further, a check of school records will show that she received no counseling for sexual abuse *prior* to the assault, and also, that her grades remained the same afterwards.

"Lastly, during the week and a half following the assault, and before Russell Swain was arrested, cell phone records will show that he received three casual calls from his daughter asking when she could visit him again."

The witness looks pleadingly to the jury, in essence, begging them to, once more, believe her and not the defense attorney.

"*No.* That's on the outside. Inside, she's hurting and hurting bad."

Bedloe responds to the woman, continuing in a calm, quiet voice, almost sympathetic. "Are you sure it's your *daughter* who is hurting?"

People in the courtroom are visibly spellbound by the emotional interactions between the defense attorney and the witness for the prosecution, and appear to be dividing into two camps defined by whom they choose to believe.

The defense attorney moves to another subject area. The crescendo continues.

"Ms. Trussoni, after Mr. Swain's behavior with your daughter, did she tell anyone? Did the girl tell you?"

The prosecution witness appears in a trance.

"Please answer the question, ma'am."

"My daughter told no one … because of embarrassment."

"Do you know how the authorities found out about it?"

She knows where he's going with this and closes her eyes in a vain attempt to escape. He answers it for her and turns to the jury to do so. Trussoni's earlier confidence is disintegrating.

"The reason Mr. Swain is where he is today, is because he voluntarily confessed his sin to a man of God, his minister."

Bedloe turns back to her.

"Is that your understanding as well?"

Again, the witness doesn't answer, her eyes now clenched tightly closed, obviously wishing for this to stop.

"You seem to have had an answer for everything else that occurred, why do you think he confessed?"

She chuckles, eyes still shut for several seconds. Then they open, and she appears calm and in control again.

"I have no idea. I'm sure *you* do though."

"Yes ma'am, I do. I would submit to you, and to the jury, that Russell Howard Swain confessed due to profound feelings of remorse and guilt."

Trussoni throws her head back, looking to the ceiling.

"Ha. Don't make me *laugh.*"

She smiles, feeling this notion can be easily brushed off as nonsense.

Bedloe walks to the witness and says,

"Jean-Paul Sartre, the famous Nobel Prize winning French existentialist philosopher and novelist, once wrote of remorse:

*'Be quiet! Anyone can spit in my face and judge me a criminal. But no one has the right to judge my remorse.'*

"Nevertheless, Russell Swain has been subjectively judged *unremorseful* by you, your family, a corrections agent for the Minnesota Department of Corrections, along with an Isanti County judge and the prosecutor at the sentencing hearing.

"What measure, what *specific* behaviors were absent that led all of you to arrive at this conclusion, declaring him to be such a totally unfeeling and unremorseful father?

"No need to answer. We'll visit that area of examination later on.

"As for feeling guilt, it is commonly looked on as 'realizing you've done something wrong and owning up to its severity, knowing the affect your bad behavior had on someone else.' *Guilt was what he suffered knowing what he had done with his daughter.*

"Ms. Trussoni, he confessed his act to a man of God for that very reason, and as can be substantiated by this minister, he was sobbing heavily while doing so. Why would he confess, and in such an emotional manner? What was there for him to gain but maybe forgiveness? And a plea for help.

"His daughter had said *nothing.*"

Trussoni immediately looks again at the jury, and laughs mockingly and loud at Bedloe's emotional explanations, in essence attempting to demonstrate it is all hogwash.

"Sir, Mr. Swain is an actor and a fraud."

"But why would he act in such a way under those circumstances? He was risking his future, his freedom. It's not logical. He *must* have been begging, crying out for someone, *anyone,* to help him deal with what he was going through. And his plea was made so this deplorable event would never happen again."

The witness continues her disinterest. Bedloe reacts.

"We obviously need to move to another subject area.

"On the day of the assault, as stated by the prosecutor during this trial, the one-five milligram diazepam pill was put into your daughter's soft drink by the defendant. Are you familiar with this medication?"

She sighs loudly. "It's a tranquilizer, a serious drug."

Bedloe goes to the jury.

"Of the several drugs medically prescribed for Mr. Swain prior to the sexual assault, one of them was diazepam, which will be examined by well qualified experts during the defense portion of the trial."

He returns to the witness.

"You stated that your daughter could easily have been *killed* by that one pill, correct?"

"Yes."

He again goes to his table and picks up another piece of paper, holds it above his head, and then reads from it.

"All right. Well, the esteemed health professionals I just mentioned, will testify that this 'killer' drug, as you referred to it, is, and I quote, 'a mild sedative medication, one that can be safely given to children over the age of *six months,*' unquote."

He throws the paper on the table, then turns back to Trussoni. Her smile is gradually disappearing. She answers softly, almost apologetically.

"I was told it was a serious drug ... by the prosecutor, before the sentencing hearing."

Bedloe moves closer.

"Right. Those people told you a lot of things you wanted to hear and you told them what they wanted to hear. Ms. Trussoni, you're an educated woman. You have a master's degree in chemistry, correct?"

"Yes."

The defense attorney then challenges the prosecution witness with a statement instead of another question.

"You knew then and you know today, that the medication given to your daughter was, in no way, life-threatening."

Trussoni does not respond. Bedloe walks to his table and picks up the 2010 sentencing hearing transcript. He opens the document to a paper clip indicating a specific page.

"Despite the fact that this pill was very mild, the judge and prosecutor at that hearing, as well as you, stated on different occasions – and I quote the statement from the judge in his final decision that clearly represented them all.

*'The selfishly placing of this drug into the defendant's daughter's soft drink, justifies the defendant receiving the maximum prison sentence.'*

Unquote." He slams the transcript shut, drops it heavily to the table with his glasses, and walks to the witness.

Trussoni scans the room, holding onto the witness stand railing. She then glares at defense counsel.

"I don't care what you say, it could've seriously injured my beautiful daughter. He *deserved* that prison sentence. Don't forget what else he did to her!"

"And by your own words, he's a potential killer who deserves to *die* in prison." Bedloe then shakes his head while looking at his watch. He wants to take a break at this time, which he considers a strategic juncture.

"Your Honor, the defense requests a forty-five-minute recess, after which I will complete my cross-examination of this witness."

Guttormsen looks at Reese-Hall.

"Objection?"

"No, Your Honor."

"Very well. The witness is advised that you will once again be on the stand. This court is in recess for forty-five minutes."

"All rise," says the bailiff, and some in the courtroom take a break as well. The rest stay, concerned they will lose their seat.

Russell Swain says quietly: "Mr. Bedloe, about what's coming up. How much tougher are you going to be on Kate?"

"Kate? Oh, Trussoni. I don't know."

Bedloe is being evasive. He called for the recess to rest briefly, to prepare to attack the witness with everything he's got. Also, he wants to give the jury a chance to recharge and be ready to resume.

Russell knows that. The preceding testimony was just to set the stage for what is to come. He grabs his attorney's forearm.

"Sir, she's one of God's children, just like you and me. Please don't hurt her any more than you already have."

Bedloe looks at Swain's hand and laughs at the comment. He's had about enough of this religious crap.

"I beg your pardon. *Me hurt her?*"

Intensely annoyed, Bedloe adds in a whisper, but with unmistakable emphasis.

"Look. What do you want? She'd *kill* you if given half a chance. And, you know that. She's trying to do and say everything she can think of, to stick a knife right between your shoulder blades!"

Bedloe forcefully pulls his arm away from his client's grip.

"I'll tell you what, why don't we all join hands and sing a hymn of love, peace, and forgiveness. Russell, this woman has put you through hell, hasn't she? Take my word for it, she won't let up. You think you've known depression before? We're in a bare-knuckled fight here, young man, and I've got to knock her out *permanently.*"

The deputy sheriff guarding Russell Swain reacts to Bedloe's anger and walks closer, so the fiery attorney immediately attempts to calm down.

Michael Swain stands outside the bar listening. Bedloe looks at him. "What about you? Do you have the stomach for this? If you don't, I'll walk into that judge's chambers right now and once again withdraw from the case!"

He knows Bedloe is in full combat mode, likes what he sees and hears. He looks at his son.

"Russ, he's got to do it. He's got to go after her. It's that or you go back to Moose Lake for thirteen more years. And don't forget, the civil suit against the medical center will be lost as well."

The defendant meekly folds his hands together on his forehead and focuses downward, stating:

"Only the power of Jesus is important. Money is insignificant."

Bedloe looks to the ceiling, then motions to Michael.

"Let's get some fresh air. We only have a few minutes left."

The two men walk out onto the lawn in back of the courthouse, away from everyone including the press. A burly, dark-skinned man who looks like he's just walked off *The Godfather* movie set, jogs up to meet Bedloe.

"Jeremiah."

"Toby. Good to see you," Bedloe says, then turns toward Swain. "This is Toby Tollefson, a private investigator who works with me every so often."

The men shake hands. A bit out of breath, Tollefson speaks to his client and old friend.

"Buddy, you got to come into the twenty-first century and get a goddamned cell phone, for Christ-sake. I'd save me a lot of time and gas money, not to mention running around trying to find you."

They both smile. Bedloe responds.

"You must've found something."

Tollefson glances at Swain, then Bedloe interjects:

"He's okay. His son is my client."

The P.I. gives him what he has.

"First of all, the prosecutor's clean. She just moved here in the last year or so. I thought you might be interested in that."

Bedloe nods his head.

"I figured as much.  What else?"

"Guttormsen's another story.  She's got relatives and friends coming out the gump-stump around here.  I've found three connections between her and the clinic ... so far."

"What?"

"Well, two of her nieces are nurses there.  Her brother-in-law's also a lawyer and president of the board of directors. And get this, Guttormsen and her husband are golfing buddies and old friends with a certain 'shrink' and his wife.  His name is in your case file, and pretty well known to you."

"All rise."

Kathryn Trussoni is again on the witness stand.

The judge speaks to her.

"Ma'am, be reminded that you are still under oath.  Mr. Bedloe, continue with your cross-examination."

Bedloe walks to the stand and stops a few feet away.  He holds a report on Klinefelter syndrome in his hand, and puts on his glasses.

"Ms. Trussoni, you stated that my client's genetic chromosomal disorder, Klinefelter syndrome, and again I quote, was 'merely a scam to avoid prison.'  You understand, of course, that genetic means he was born with it, right? How much do you know about this disorder?"

She answers sharply.

"More than you *think* I know."

The prosecutor stands.

"Your Honor, objection. I have a hunch that defense counsel is going to provide us with a potentially redundant litany of all the things *his* witnesses will relate during the defense portion of this trial."

Judge Guttormsen responds.

"Mr. Bedloe, are you sure cross-examination about this Klinefelter business is necessary?"

He nods his agreement with Reese-Hall.

"The prosecutor makes a good point. The defense wishes to abandon questioning the witness's knowledge concerning my client's Klinefelter syndrome.

"Because Ms. Trussoni is such a self-professed expert on this matter, it would appear unnecessary to enlighten her about what *our* expert witnesses will have to say. The jury will hear that soon enough."

He throws the report on his table, then walks to the jury and takes off the glasses, rubbing his eyes with thumb and index finger. He roughly combs his hair with the fingers of his other hand.

"Ladies and gentlemen, my client and I deeply appreciate your continued attention, for there is a vital need to reconstruct an objective portrait of this family tragedy."

He turns and goes back to the prosecution witness, and opens up another area he wants to examine.

"Ma'am, the solid bond between a mother and her daughter is a sacred and emotional one. Might we, at least, agree on that?"

"Yes. Most definitely."

"Good. So, if a mother testifies under oath in a court of law, knowing that while doing so, what she's been saying about her daughter's ordeal for all these many years, is untrue, couldn't that testimony then be interpreted as being self-serving and have little or nothing to do with this girl?"

"What are you implying? I used my daughter? For the love of God, I would *never* do that to her."

"You stated in this very courtroom that Russell Swain is a sexual predator, and that he had sexually assaulted his daughter for years, along with other minor females as well."

Bedloe goes to the jury.

"Is there a greater defamatory charge that one adult can level against another, than being unjustly accused of, and thereafter, branded for life as a *sexual predator* of children – including one's *own child?*"

Turning and walking back and forth to face everyone in the gallery, he places clenched fists hard against his midsection.

"Can't all of us in this courtroom grasp the feeling in our gut upon being labeled such a thing?  Personally, I cannot even *imagine* the reaction I would have if this *despicable* charge was leveled against me.

"What type of person would say such a damnable thing as this, knowing the allegations are false?"

He returns to the witness.

"And, it didn't stop there.  My client was also referred to again and again as *a threat to society.*

"These two slanderous charges were made by you, and to date, have not been substantiated with any evidence, only your word.  Ms. Trussoni, no decent and honest adult human being would *ever* state such charges against another human being without absolute confirmation of facts to validate them. Especially not in a *court of law.*"

Bedloe glances at the judge, then goes to his table and picks up two reports, one in each hand, and returns to the witness while addressing the court.

"Your Honor, these two reports are marked for identification, defense exhibits six and seven, and will be further explained during the defense portion of the trial."

Guttermsen nods, accepting the defense documents. Bedloe holds up one of the reports.

"This report was written by a forensic psychologist."

He holds up the other.  "And, the one I hold in this hand was written by a clinical psychologist.

"Both clearly state that the defendant is *not* a sexual predator and is *not* a threat to society. They will testify to this fact under oath later on."

He places the reports back on the table and returns to the witness.

"To my knowledge, there is no evidence to state otherwise.

"So, what it comes down to, is the fact that two respected professionals thoroughly and objectively examined my client and informed the court at the 2010 sentencing hearing of their findings. It is our contention that the court either manipulated those findings to suit their best interests, or *completely* ignored them."

He walks to the jury, pointing directly at the witness.

"In addition to these reports, Ms. Trussoni's *written* victim impact statement was given to the court *prior* to the sentencing hearing as well. Therefore, it knew of its damaging contents before her oral presentation."

Bedloe makes a show of reaching into his back pocket and extracting his wallet. He holds it above his head, waving it back and forth.

"I'll bet my last dollar that the court used this woman's victim impact statement filled with lies, to guarantee no outcome other than imprisonment would prevail.

"Everything was stacked against Russell Swain from the start. There was no way this man was not going to prison."

Judge Guttormsen is speechless. The prosecutor stands.

"Your Honor, Mr. Bedloe has made some serious allegations against this court, with no evidence to substantiate them!"

Bedloe responds, but laughs while again pointing to the witness.

"Yet, this court continues to allow devastating charges to be made by Kathryn Trussoni against Russell Swain, with *no* evidence substantiating any of her claims."

The prosecutor sits, shaking her head in exaggerated frustration, and the judge continues to remain silent. Bedloe returns to the witness.

"The outcome of that hearing and sentence that resulted, were clearly prearranged, and being aware of your hatred of the defendant, you ma'am, were manipulated to 'drive the final nail into your former husband's coffin.'"

"That's stupid," she shoots back.

"Really? Let's see what else was said during that hearing in 2010 and again today."


"You have stated that if Mr. Swain is released from prison and admitted to Alpha, everyone in your family will be unable to remain in their homes. In fact, you will all have to go into hiding. Therefore, he *must* remain in prison. Correct?"

She feels uneasy, not knowing the direction of this question but finally says, "Yes, we'd all have to move."

"That's not what I asked. I'm talking about hiding, going incognito."

"What?"

"Move where he can't find you and your family, including his daughter, and change your appearances."

"Yes. He'll be free, and might only have to wear an ankle monitor."

Bedloe ignores her manipulation of the response.

"As a result, along with your use of the term, *sexual predator*, your fear is that Mr. Swain could easily *prey* on your entire extended family, suggesting he would do bodily harm.

"And that your mother, as you stated in the victim impact statement in 2010 and here today, is especially fearful of him, and fears for her life if he is free to receive treatment in lieu of prison. Correct?"

"*Yes*. She is."

"Did your mother appear before the sentencing hearing?"

"No."

"Did she write a letter to the judge?"

"No."

"Will any member of the extended Trussoni family come before this court and swear under oath, that the defendant has ever verbally made threats or has actually done bodily harm?"

The witness pauses momentarily, and nods repeatedly. Then she shakes her head back and forth.

Bedloe continues, not needing an oral response.

"Ma'am, I do not care to personally dig up skeletons from anyone's family closet. However, I do wish to spend another brief moment discussing your mother."

The prosecutor objects.

"Your Honor, the witness' mother is not relevant to this case."

Judge Guttormsen looks at Bedloe, who responds quickly because he is sure the objection will be sustained.

"If another vital decision concerning the future of Russell Swain is now to be made by a jury, they must have all the evidence. The witness has already testified in this courtroom about her mother's fear of my client."

"Proceed, counsel. Carefully."

"Ms. Trussoni, with due respect concerning your mother, I'll ask you but one question, and then permanently exclude her from this trial."

She has no idea where Bedloe's going.

"Does your mother have a history of psychiatric disorders, and continues to remain under a doctor's care for them?"

She sits shocked at the question and looks straight ahead. The prosecutor stands to object.

"Your Honor, a doctor-patient relationship is privileged information. The witness does not have to answer."

Bedloe responds directly to Reese-Hall.

"My question is a general one. I am not asking for specifics, just a 'yes' or 'no'. However, if the witness refuses to answer, the defense could subpoena her mother's records by filing a civil law suit against the witness for reasons already established, which we are prepared to do."

Judge Guttormsen looks sympathetically, yet sternly at the witness. "Ms. Trussoni, it appears to be in your best interest to answer defense counsel's question."

After a moment, she nods slightly with head down, and Bedloe responds.

"Let the record show that the witness answered in the affirmative."

The judge states: "So noted."

Bedloe acknowledges the ruling. He looks at Kathryn Trussoni, almost to the point of pity, and is quite aware that she is not only exploiting her daughter, but also her own mother.

And, it's now crystal clear as to why.

He walks to face the jury, still addressing the witness for the prosecution.

The building crescendo is about to reach its peak.

"From late 2008 until January 11, 2010, the day of Russell Swain's arrest, were you and the defendant in the midst of a battle for permanent custody of your daughter?"

"Yes, but he …"

"What was the wish of your daughter during that time?"

Trussoni looks nervously around the courtroom. Again, there is no response. Bedloe knows she is carefully picking and choosing when to answer, and when not to. He again answers it for her, knowing she won't be truthful, especially concerning this issue.

"Your daughter's wish was to permanently relocate from your home in Winona, Minnesota, where she has lived with you since the divorce almost a decade ago, and move to Cambridge, Minnesota to live with her father and his newly blended family. Isn't that correct?"

"No, that is *not* correct."

Bedloe goes back to face her at close range.

"This fact is verifiable by Mr. Thomas Kraft, my client's attorney at that time, who handled the custody battle for your former husband. Your attorney can easily be subpoenaed to appear at this trial, verifying that as well."

She then answers just above a whisper, her face is expressionless, yet with eyes clearly filled with fear.

"He brainwashed her, he … he …"

The judge addresses the witness.

"Ma'am, please speak loud enough so the jury can hear you."

Trussoni looks meekly at the judge, and then toward the jury, clearly begging for their sympathy. Her vocal pitch rises an octave above normal for the woman, nearly that of a little girl.

"I said, he brain-brainwashed her, that-that's what. He got her to-to hate me. He's very good at that, don't you know … lying and manipulating."

Bedloe figures it should be very clear to everyone by now, that this latest performance is just another deceptive ploy.

Surprisingly, the woman then looks at Michael Swain, and her authentic person instantly reappears. The vocal pitch returns to normal, the stammer evaporates. She wags her index finger at her former father-in-law and says, matter-of-factly:

"Michael Swain can tell you. His father, Michael Swain there, he can tell you. I was once told by him that his son could sell snowballs to Eskimos. He did the same to my beautiful daughter, by lying and manipulated her into hating me. Her own mother.

"That man turned my daughter against me. She doesn't *hate* me, she *loves* me."

Bedloe then goes to the sole reason for Trussoni's testimony today and in 2010. He returns to his table and gestures to an open display of several folders outlining his client's medical history.

"Ms. Trussoni, these are Russell Swain's medical records from five different clinics, in both Wisconsin and Minnesota from 1990 to the end of 2009, just prior to his incarceration in the Isanti County Jail." He picks up one and walks back to the witness.

"This report is from the MidState Medical Center for the year 2009. As written by two psychiatrists at the center, Mr. Swain was being treated for prolonged, severe clinical depression."

He then points to the other medical reports.

"None of these indicate treatment for a serious psychological condition before that time. *Not one.*

"The MidState Medical Center report *specifically* substantiates that his debilitating depression was due predominately to your ongoing sadistic assault against him once his daughter informed you of her wish to live with him and his family. And it continues today, *in a court of law.*

"This torment you perpetrated against your former husband, resulting from his daughter's wish, and the hell you put him through, is well documented. Would you care to read what the psychiatrists wrote?"

She shakes her head in crazed exaggeration. The prosecutor slowly stands, attempting to momentarily break the tension.

"Your Honor, is this report a matter of court record?"

Bedloe reacts angrily to the interruption before Judge Guttormsen has a chance to respond.

"It is defense exhibit number nine, Madam Prosecutor, *and you damn well know it.*"

The prosecutor sits. The judge does not respond. Bedloe goes back to the witness.

"There are at *least* three very credible witnesses who will voluntarily appear before the court, and testify concerning the level to which you *despise* your former husband and how you would do *anything* to destroy him."

He moves closer, all of a sudden feeling light-headed, yet continues.

"Your daughter had been a witness to this disturbing generalized pattern of manipulative and verbal aggression against her father for some time. And, the reason for your behavior?"

Defense counsel tightly grips the witness stand railing, exhausted.

"*Because your daughter wanted to live with her dad and his family – and not you.*"

He then slowly walks to his table, but suddenly turns back to her. His face is pale, and his eyes are bloodshot.

"One last thing. Russell Swain strongly suggested to his daughter, that *nothing* be mentioned to you about the happy things that occurred when she was with him and his family, because they both knew how it would be twisted and distorted to suit your vendetta, which was solely for the purpose of turning her against him.

"That's why she wouldn't answer you. It had *nothing* to do with sexual behavior. This devoted twelve-year old girl was trying to protect herself and her father from *your selfish wrath-filled attempt to destroy their relationship.*"

Trussoni responds directly to the jury, smiling. Her arms extend to them with palms up, almost in sacrifice.

"Don't you see what's going on here? He's trying to turn the whole thing around, and make it appear it was *me* that caused him to rape his own daughter. Please see that."

She then turns to Bedloe with explosive anger, but points to Russell Swain. *"You're no better than him."*

Prosecutor Reese-Hall jumps to her feet.

"Your Honor, I request an adjournment until tomorrow, at which time ..."

Judge Guttormsen interrupts her.

"We will continue until counsel has completed his examination of this witness, even if it goes well beyond noon."

Emotionally depleted, the defense attorney returns to his table. With head down, he turns to address the bench.

"Your Honor, the defense has completed its cross-examination of this prosecution witness."


Silence envelops the packed courtroom. Cognitive dissonance is clearly felt. No one is able to make eye contact with Kathryn Trussoni. The sympathetic attention that was once accorded her, is now replaced with confusion and conflict.

The prosecutor speaks quietly, still seated, and like Bedloe, is equally near emotional limits.

"There will be no redirect. The prosecution rests."

Judge Guttormsen addresses the witness without looking at her.

"Ma'am, you are excused."

She remains seated momentarily, maintaining the same haunting smile. Yet, her eyes are able to exhibit the continued expression of hatred, not only for Russell Swain, but now for Jeremiah Bedloe as well.

The judge glances at the woman, and waits for a few more moments, then announces:

"This court is adjourned until two p.m. this afternoon, at which time the defense portion of the trial will begin."

And the bailiff nervously states:

"All rise."


The witness, still on the stand, raises both hands to her head, and tightly fills her fingers with hair. She cries out with a deafening shrill scream:

*"This is madness. Madness."*

She stares murderously at her former husband, while the psychotic vendetta continues in the midst of a startled courtroom. In fear, Russell Swain doesn't have the courage to look back at her as the screaming continues.

*"You're not her father. You never were her father. My daughter is of my blood, not yours. She's mine. Mine. You will not take her from me. I'll kill you first."*

The woman promptly scans the entire stone-faced audience, suddenly understanding what was just said. Then her frantic gaze returns to the jury, and now in a calm and normal voice – a shift almost as disturbing as her shouting, appeals one last time.

"He's a rapist. Don't you see what he is?"

Realizing her pleas are now having little effect, she slowly and calmly picks up her purse and opens it.

The threat to kill the defendant causes the nearest deputy sheriff to quickly rush and seize the bag to double check its contents. He shakes his head to the judge, indicating there is no weapon, then hands it back to the witness. Trussoni extracts a set of keys, smiling strangely at Bedloe and her ex-husband. She stands tall and walks out of the courtroom looking neither left nor right, acknowledging no one.

Once she's gone, Judge Guttormsen, as overcome as anyone, bangs her gavel. "We've seen and heard about enough for one day. This court is adjourned, and will reconvene tomorrow morning at nine a.m. The defense will then present its first witness."

## Scene Four

# Witnesses for the Defense

*After Tuesday's court session, Bedloe is still feeling extreme fatigue during dinner with Michael Swain. Swain notices it and suggests the trial be delayed one day so his son's attorney can get some needed rest. Bedloe stubbornly refuses.*

*However, when he returns to the motel, there is a driving need to get in his rental car and visit a Cambridge liquor store. Knowing from years of experience what the craving is all about, and because of a deep respect for his client and his profession, Bedloe enters his room and takes a couple of sleeping pills instead. He closes the window blinds and goes to bed right away.*

*Eight-thirty, Wednesday morning.*

The two men are driving to the courthouse in Swain's truck. Earlier, during breakfast, he excitedly told Bedloe of a national telecast Tuesday night concerning the case but only caught the tail-end of it, so he didn't know much about what was reported on.

As they get close to the courthouse, both are startled at what they see. Swain immediately drives to a private county parking lot in the rear of the building, luckily finding a space.

They quickly get out and run to the rear door and knock.  An employee answers, and they successfully duck into the building without anyone seeing them.


A national television news network had aired a recorded portion of the heated cross-examination of Trussoni by Bedloe. It was undoubtedly leaked by a spectator in the gallery using a cellular telephone.  Following the emotional excerpts, a T.V. guest panel discussed what transpired in the courtroom, and whether or not freedom for the child rapist, Russell Swain, was acceptable or unacceptable.  The program included the fact that the victim was the defendant's daughter.

Since that telecast, a number of media satellite trucks on state and national level are steadily increasing and lining the streets near the courthouse.  A number of reporters are clutching microphones, asking questions of city officials as to what may unfold during today's court session. Local residents are also being asked about their opinions on the case.

Those in the courtroom can hear the muffled sounds of mostly female voices outside, protestors loudly chanting their opposition to sexual assault, and swift, sure punishment for perpetrators.  Both men and women are carrying placards denouncing domestic violence and child abuse.

The county immediately bans all cameras, cellular devices, and lap top computers from the courtroom.  Sheriff's deputies search everyone entering the building.  Only media, holding pen and paper, are allowed into the trial.

Again, Lorna and Victor stand against the back wall. The courtroom is now standing room only.

"All rise."

Judge Guttormsen enters and sits. She appears very nervous.

Russell Swain is already seated beside his attorney. The judge starts the proceedings.

"The defense will call its first witness."

Bedloe responds. "We call Dr. Paul Lagerfeldt."

The man enters and walks to the witness stand.


*Lagerfeldt is in his early- to mid-fifties, with a crew-cut and dressed in casual slacks and an open-collared sport shirt.*

*He has been a respected forensic psychologist for thirty years, and is regarded as a leading authority on sexual offenders. His work also includes close dealings with Alpha Human Services.*


The bailiff swears him in.

"Raise your right hand. Do you swear to tell the truth, the whole truth, and nothing but the truth?"

"I will."

"Please be seated."

Bedloe walks to the witness stand.

"Dr. Lagerfeldt, you are a forensic psychologist licensed in the state of Minnesota, is that correct?"

"Yes, I am."

"You were hired and paid by the defendant, Russell Howard Swain, to interview him and administer psychological tests prior to his court sentencing hearing in 2010, correct?"

"That is correct."

"And, was a portion of that total evaluation to determine his psychological state?"

"It was."

"Was it also for the purpose of making recommendations to the court at that sentencing hearing?"

"Yes."

"First of all, please tell the jury what evaluation process was used."

The witness faces the ten people in the jury box.

"I interviewed Mr. Swain twice and also administered two psychological tests, the Minnesota Multi-phasic Personality Inventory and the Multi-phasic Sex Inventory. Both tests are standardized and used by most forensic psychologists in the United States. I visited him a total of four times."

"Were all of the visits, as you referred to them, while Mr. Swain was incarcerated in the Isanti County Jail?"

"They were."

"Do you recall the month?"

"Yes, it was during the month of February, 2010."

"Now once the evaluation process was completed, please inform the jury as to what your final recommendations were."

"It was my recommendation that he be sent to the sexual offender residential treatment center at Alpha Human Services in Minneapolis in lieu of prison."

"How long does the treatment last?"

"Two to three years."

"As stated in your report, the Alpha program would also address related psychological factors that may have led to the crime, other than sexual matters?"

"Yes, very much so. May I add something else here?"

"Go ahead."

"Although retained by a defendant, it should also be noted, that my final recommendation to a court has often been that a client be remanded to the Minnesota Department of Corrections for incarceration. However, this certainly was *not* the case with Mr. Swain."

"So, based on the total findings, what were your final conclusions as they applied to his criminal offense?"

"Well, first of all, Mr. Swain is not considered to be a sexual predator. I might say that Alpha Human Services, which also did an analysis of him, basically concurred with my assessment. Secondly, the science of risk prediction for him was that he had a low likelihood of sexual recidivism with treatment and proper supervision. Lastly, he was not regarded as a threat to public safety."

"That was in 2010, what about now?"

"If he has not committed a similar offense while in prison, it would remain the same."

"He has not. Doctor, it is my understanding that you conduct a program in conjunction with Alpha Human Services, that offers joint therapy to a daughter or son and a parent offender, and this usually commences towards the conclusion of treatment and confinement at Alpha. Is that correct?"

"Yes. And, it has been very successful."

"In your professional opinion, sir, would Mr. Swain be a candidate for that program if he were to be admitted to Alpha?"

"He certainly would."

Bedloe thanks Dr. Lagerfeldt, and then says to Judge Guttormsen:

"Your Honor, I have concluded my questioning of this witness, subject to redirect."

The judge looks at Janet Reese-Hall.

"The prosecution may proceed with cross-examination."

She starts to question the witness from her table.

"Dr. Lagerfeldt, the defense has kind of tip-toed around the totality of the evaluation you made of the defendant. Let's get a little more specific."

She walks to the witness.

"What information did you have with which to prepare yourself for the meetings with Mr. Swain? Specifically, the interviews, not the tests."

"I had the charges against him, I had police reports. He had no psychological history, so I did not have that. I reviewed all the documents that Mr. Swain's first attorney provided to me, so then I interviewed him."

"You had no psychological history of the defendant?"

"No."

"Doctor, during the sentencing hearing in 2010, didn't you state that the defendant had symptoms of psychological disorders and named them all?"

"Yes. I noted definite symptoms. But, what I was given by his first attorney included no history. These symptoms were what Mr. Bedloe was referring to minutes ago."

"I see, so you felt the defendant showed definite symptoms of psychological disorders. Do you happen to recall what the disorders were?"

"From recollection, I'd say they were bipolar affective disorder with both depression and mania, along with schizoaffective disorder, adult antisocial and narcissistic personality disorders, suicidal ideation, and there were clear symptoms of chemical dependency."

Bedloe is stunned at the last disorder listed by the psychologist, and feels a sudden rush of excitement. Surprisingly, the prosecutor continues, perhaps not recalling the list of defense witnesses submitted at pretrial.

"Chemical dependency? Alcohol, drugs, what?"

"I couldn't fully determine, probably drugs."

"Then how could you make that professional determination if you're not certain?"

"In listening to him respond, he appeared disoriented, confused, and lost. I've seen my share of drug addicts during my thirty-year career, you know."

"But these were observations. As defense counsel earlier found when questioning a prosecution witness, no blood or urine samples were taken and therefore examined, correct?"

"To my knowledge, there were no tests done."

"Dr. Lagerfeldt, what about sexual disorders? Could you determine if Mr. Swain had any of those?"

"I suspected he had a sexual disorder, possibly paraphilias – in other words, obsessed or fixated on various objects or things regarding sex.

"And, I knew at the time of the interview that he was an incestuous pedophile."

"We all know of the incest, doctor.  The defendant has already admitted to that."

Bedloe stands.  "Objection."

The judge responds.

"On what basis, Mr. Bedloe?  Your client previously pleaded guilty to this charge."

"First of all, the county has no evidence substantiating that intercourse occurred, only my client's questionable confession. Secondly, the minor is not his biological daughter.  Therefore, if intercourse did occur, it is not incestuous."

Guttormsen asks Bedloe, while also looking at the media in the back of the courtroom:

"Counsel, would you please inform the court how you came to the conclusion concerning incest?"

"By reading Minnesota Statute 609.36."

He holds up a sheet of paper.  Guttormsen appears unsettled. Bedloe continues.

"May I read it, Your Honor?"

"No, you may not.  The court is familiar with the statute, and has determined the minor female in this case *is* his daughter."

"But it clearly states ..."

"Sir, the court is already *clear* on what it states."

Bedloe bangs his index finger hard against the table in anger.

*"Exception.* This distinction *must* be included."

"I beg your pardon. *Must* be? May I remind counsel who occupies this chair?"

Defense counsel responds louder, "I said exception, Your Honor!"

"As mentioned so often, Mr. Bedloe, this court will not tolerate emotional outbursts of any kind. And incidentally, your objection is overruled as well."

"Is my exception noted?"

"It is noted."

Judge Guttormsen looks to the prosecutor. "Proceed."

"Dr. Lagerfeldt, during the sentencing hearing, *that* prosecutor informed you that Mr. Swain had previous victims. You were visibly surprised, were you not?"

"Yes. I believe Mr. Swain may have lied to me then. During our interviews, he said his daughter was the only one."

Bedloe is again on his feet. He looks directly at Reese-Hall.

"Objection. Dr. Lagerfeldt was told *after* the 2010 hearing that there were other victims by the previous prosecutor, not *during.*

"This bogus information supposedly came from the Alpha Human Services intake summary prepared by Douglas Wilson. However, *nowhere* in his report does Mr. Wilson say the females were *victims*.

"Ms. Reese-Hall is attempting to mislead the jury by trying to substantiate what the defense has already refuted. The females in question were not victims. *Period.*"

Bedloe looks directly at the forensic psychologist.

"In other words, doctor, you were lied to by the prosecutor in 2010, not by my client during your interviews with him prior to that hearing."

Reese-Hall responds, slightly embarrassed. "Your Honor, defense counsel is correct. I withdraw my question concerning previous victims."

Guttormsen, however, looks nervously at the jury, and then at Bedloe. She's conflicted.

"Mr. Bedloe, you are being given great latitude here. Do not, sir, abuse the court's generosity. In additional to the prosecutor's withdrawal, the jury is also instructed to disregard the last response from defense counsel, and it will be stricken from the record. Proceed, Madam Prosecutor."

Jeremiah Bedloe sits and leans back in his chair, extending his arms and looks to the ceiling.

"Great latitude? Generosity? I don't believe this."

Guttormsen does not respond.

Reese-Hall glares at her. For the first time, she questions the judge's past rulings concerning the defense's objections. It was conceded that Bedloe's last objection was clearly substantiated, and now acknowledges the possibility that the judge may be exhibiting preference towards the prosecution in furtherance of some agenda.

The prosecutor senses the possibility that an impartial pursuit of justice is being replaced with political or social expediency, but she works to dismiss such thoughts from her mind and concentrate on the trial.

"Dr. Lagerfeldt - - we were talking about the sexual disorders the defendant has. In the psychosexual evaluation that you wrote, it elaborately depicted his sexual history, did it not?"

"Yes, it did."

"Did you, by any chance, bring that report with you?"

"No, I did not."

"Well, let me refresh your memory. In it, you wrote that the defendant admitted to having sex with men and animals. And also, that he had been involved in sadomasochist sex and bondage. Do you recall that?"

"Yes. However, he didn't state these things to me. They were all confessed to his minister and later written in the Isanti County report, which I then included in mine."

"All right. He also went on to state that he became sexually aroused while watching a film about a sadistic serial killer who enjoyed having sex with a woman before killing her. Do you recall that?"

"Yes, but again that was in the other reports, not mine."

"After all these disclosures to others, he did admit to *you* having incestuous intercourse."

Bedloe stands again, appearing weary. His voice is quiet and unemotional.

"Objection. The prosecutor's aware that the court overruled my objection concerning the use of the term, *incest*. As a result, I've got a feeling this socially forbidden behavior is going to be thrown into the mix of questions as often as she can. If she does, the defense must be allowed to counter with the Minnesota statute that defines incest as *a sexual act between members of a biological, blood family*."

The prosecutor responds before the judge has the opportunity.

"Your Honor, defense has found a way to include the *supposed* legal definition, however, the court and the jury should be made aware that Dr. Lagerfeldt stated in his psychosexual report on a number of occasions, that the victim in this case is, in fact, the defendant's *biological* daughter."

Judge Guttormsen looks at Bedloe for a response. He looks at Reese-Hall.

"For Pete's sake, we've already *gone* through all this with Trussoni during her testimony before this court."

The defense attorney nods to the witness. "With all due respect to Dr. Lagerfeldt, he is mistaken." Counsel then faces Guttormsen.

"Your Honor, as was alluded to during the prosecution phase of this trial, my client has a genetic disorder called 47, XXY, also known as Klinefelter syndrome. Nowhere in the doctor's report does he mention this."

The prosecutor looks at Bedloe, clearly puzzled. "What does *that* have to do with anything?"

Jeremiah Bedloe looks down and puts a hand on his client's shoulder.

"Russell Swain has a genetic condition that, in his case, and in almost all cases, results in the post-pubertal male being completely sterile. He cannot have children. As a result, his daughter was conceived by artificial insemination.

"The girl is not his biological daughter, therefore, *it is not incest.*"

Tears form in Swain's eyes. Bedloe glances at the jury.

"This genetic disorder will be the next topic examined by the defense."

The jury looks at the defendant. After a moment, Guttormsen speaks very coldly.

"The court will take the matter of the term, *incest,* under advisement. For the time being, Madam Prosecutor, please refrain from using that term until I have ruled."

The prosecutor nods and deliberately does not vocally respond, except to angrily state:

"I am done with this witness."

"Mr. Bedloe, redirect?"

"Yes, Your Honor."

He gets up and stands at his table. "Doctor, in your response to the prosecution's question concerning psychological disorders present in Mr. Swain when he was evaluated in 2010, you stated symptoms of schizoaffective and bipolar affective disorders. Correct?"

"Yes."

"Isn't a fact that if these two disorders are present simultaneously in a person, the common result would be hallucinations and delusions?

"Very much so."

"You also stated that Mr. Swain showed symptoms of drug dependency."

"That is correct."

The defense attorney walks to the jury. "I ask that you, the jury, please keep these points in mind during testimony presented later on by other defense witnesses."

He turns and speaks to Dr. Lagerfeldt while walking to stand in front of him.

"Finally, doctor, do you recall the defendant mentioning the meeting he had with his minister, William McCord, a week or so after he assaulted his daughter?"

"Vaguely. Please refresh."

"Gladly. At that meeting, which was included in your report as well as others, it stated that Mr. Swain told his minister everything prosecutor Reese-Hall just mentioned – sex with animals, sex with men, involvement in sadomasochism, etc.

"Later on, Mr. Swain recanted those claims to you, did he not?"

"Yes, he did."

"In your thirty years of experience with sex offenders, why would he make those claims if they were not true? Mr. Swain was trying to be a mentor for his church's Men's Sober Home, a program assisting alcohol- and drug-addicted people, something he truly wanted to do. Surely he would have known those disclosures to the minister would doom any possibility of him being accepted."

"I can only suggest probable motivations, none of which can now be substantiated, I would imagine."

"Is there any evidence to show that the behaviors mentioned in these particular confessions – *including* the criminal charge against him – had actually *occurred* other than by his saying that they did?"

"Not to my knowledge."

Bedloe looks at Russell, and then turns to face the jury. He addresses Lagerfeldt.

"Doctor, the prosecution witnesses, both in 2010 and during this trial, have accused Mr. Swain of being socially deviant, a predator, and a threat to society. All of these claims have been refuted by Alpha Human Services and yourself.

"Let me ask you *again*. In your opinion, did my client ever actually *do* the things he has confessed to?"

The witness pauses to think, then answers.

"I cannot address the intercourse. But as to the other behaviors? No. In my professional opinion, he did not."

Bedloe dramatically turns back to him.

"Why then, in your professional opinion, did he say these things? Why would he tell all those lies?"

"I believe Mr. Swain was out of control. They were a cry for help."

"In conclusion, sir, do you continue to stand by this man, and your professional assessment of him?"

The forensic psychologist responds quite emotionally.

"Yes. It is frustrating to see Russell Swain languish in prison. The judge at the sentencing hearing ignored or distorted many of the findings I presented in my report."

"Dr. Lagerfeldt, have you recently had other cases, ones more severe than his, whereby the men were sent to Alpha in lieu of prison?"

"Yes. Particularly within just the past year, I have had at least four cases of fathers who were incestuous pedophiles, and were referred for indeterminate civil commitment. The county attorneys involved in each one followed my analysis that these individuals were amenable to treatment and could be referred to Alpha House.

"Each of them had many more than just one victim."

With a sympathetic smile, he looks at the incarcerated man.

"It is unfortunate that there is not consistency and objectivity in our state when it comes to cases of sexual offenders."

"Thank you, doctor. Your Honor, I have no further questions."

Judge Guttormsen responds.

"Sir, thank you for appearing. Mr. Bedloe, your next witness."

"The defense now calls Mr. Douglas Wilson."

He enters the courtroom and is sworn in.


*Douglas Wilson is an athletic looking young man, approximately in his late twenties to early thirties. He has longish curly brown hair and a rugged-looking mustache and beard.*

"Mr. Wilson, please state your occupational title and present place of employment."

"I am the Director of Intake and Outpatient Services at Alpha Human Services, based in Minneapolis."

"You are a licensed psychologist, is that correct?"

"Yes. A clinical psychologist."

"Why is it that you do not refer to yourself as *doctor*?"

"Personal choice, although I have a Ph.D."

"Fair enough. During late winter of 2010, you conducted a pre-entry interview to determine if Russell Swain would be an appropriate candidate for your inpatient sexual offender treatment program, correct?"

"That is correct."

"Sir, please inform the jury what your findings were."

"That Mr. Swain was considered an acceptable candidate for placement in the residential program should the court place him on probation, and should he be able to pay the cost of the program."

"It is obviously a fact that at the sentencing hearing, Mr. Swain was not granted probation to attend your program. However, prior to that, did he and his family state to you that they would or would not be able to pay for the fees?"

"They mentioned it would create a financial hardship, but would be able to."

"So, he was all set to go. At no cost to the state."

"Yes."

"Now, moving on to your questioning as to Mr. Swain's past behaviors, he was asked if he had ever engaged in various sexual acts deemed either illegal or culturally unacceptable. Do you have a list with you of what those 'acts' are?"

"Yes."

"What are they?"

"Overall, Mr. Swain was asked if he had ever engaged in cross-dressing, group sex, the use of force to gain sex, the use of bondage or restraints, or the use of 1-900 phone lines."

"You stated those from memory. These are standard questions your agency utilizes?"

"Yes."

"What were his responses?"

"He denied using any of them."

"Thank you, Mr. Wilson. No further questions, Your Honor. However, as before, subject to redirect."

The judge looks at the prosecutor

"Madam Prosecutor, cross-examination?"

Reese-Hall stands at her table.

"Yes, Your Honor. Mr. Wilson, isn't it true that Mr. Swain informed you he spied on female classmates while in high school?"

"Yes."

"Also, that he engaged in voyeurism on neighbors while in the sixth and eighth grade?"

"Yes."

"That he engaged in exhibitionism by running naked across a football field when in high school?"

"Yes."

"And lastly, that he had solicited prostitutes, three of them, as I recall!"

"Yes."

"No further questions."

Reese-Hall sits. Bedloe stands for redirect. The judge addresses him.

"Mr. Bedloe, will this take long? The court must adjourn early this morning due to a prior commitment."

"This will take but a minute or two. My redirect is a response to the prosecutor's questions, not to ask Mr. Wilson any new ones. However, sir, feel free to refute anything I say if it is incorrect.

"Russell Swain graduated from high school in 1985. With the exception of the prostitutes, all behaviors just listed occurred *before* that time, some *twenty-five years* prior to the January 2, 2010 sexual assault.  There is no record of any other criminal complaints or charges filed against my client, before or after, until 2010."  He glances at the prosecutor.

"And incidentally, that scamper across the football field was at one o'clock in the morning, and in the company of other nude teenagers."

Bedloe goes on addressing the witness.

"Lastly, the prostitutes solicited by Mr. Swain were during the time he served in the United States Marine Corps from 1985 through 1987.  This included two prostitutes in Thailand and one in Nevada.  For the record, he was single at the time, and all three were consenting adult females."

He looks to the witness.  "Mr. Wilson, any rebuttal?"

Wilson shakes his head.  "No."

"Your Honor, I have completed my examination."

Judge Guttormsen nods to defense counsel, then looks at the witness.

"Thank you for your testimony, Mr. Wilson.  This court is adjourned until this afternoon at one-thirty, at which time the defense will call its next witness."

"All rise."


The judge leaves and the people in the courtroom start to file out as well.  Jeremiah Bedloe turns to find Lorna but she is nowhere in sight. He sits and starts to stuff papers back into the briefcases.

A deputy sheriff walks over to take Russell Swain back to his cell. Bedloe asks for a few minutes with his client. The officer nods and stands back five or six feet.

Michael Swain gets up and walks to the gate in the bar that separates the trial participants and the spectator's gallery to be with his son for a few moments. He gestures for the deputy's permission, which he grants with a nod. Bedloe speaks to Russell.

"How are you holding up?"

"Okay."

"Good."

"Mr. Bedloe, what's next?"

"Klinefelter syndrome."

Father approaches son, who stands and they briefly embrace. An older, rather attractive woman walks through the gate and goes to hug Russell. The deputy recognizes her, and allows the exchange.

Russell looks at his attorney.

"Sir, I'd like you to meet my mom, Diane Schuller."

Pleasantly surprised, he stands and extends his hand.

"Well, nice to finally meet you. I was wondering when I'd have the pleasure."

Schuller walks closer to the defense attorney and ignores the hand. Instead, she gives him a big hug and starts to cry.

"Excuse me, Mr. Bedloe, I'm just a little overwhelmed by all this."

"That's okay. Listen, I'll reserve a seat for you next to Michael."

"No, thank you, I'm here with my husband and sister. We're alright where we are."

"As a matter of fact, my request isn't because I'm an altruistic soul. It's to show family support for your son. Hell, if possible, bring the whole damn extended family!"

Her disposition abruptly changes and responds a bit coolly. "No, thank you."

Bedloe is disappointed and puzzled, but smiles. Schuller stiffly reciprocates, then walks to her son. They both immediately join hands and bow their heads. With their eyes closed tightly, she prepares to pray.

Bedloe glances at Michael Swain, who looks back at the attorney with an abashed smile and shrugs his shoulders.

"Dear Lord, we ask that You bless us all," she says aloud, "And through Your mercy, bring my son and our family peace on this earth, until we join You in the Heavenly world prepared for us. May You bring the wisdom of the Holy Spirit into Mr. Bedloe, and guide him through this terrible ordeal. In the name of Jesus, Your Son and our Lord. Amen."

Russell Swain's response is soft and emotional.

"Amen, thank you, dear Lord. All praise and glory to Your name."

The deputy sheriff moves in and accompanies Russell back to his cell.

Bedloe looks at Michael Swain.

"Let's get some lunch."

The two men sit at a table in a small out-of-the-way downtown Cambridge greasy-spoon, discussing what occurred that morning. They have gotten to know each other quite well. Swain, as Bedloe expects, orders a chicken salad sandwich on wheat and decaffeinated coffee. Bedloe, as Swain expects, orders a bacon and cheese hamburger with French fries and a chocolate milk shake. Each smile at the other's selection.

They continue eating and talking, when a large, unshaven middle-aged man walks up with heavy steel-toed work boots against the wooden floor of the restaurant announcing his arrival. He's wearing a Minnesota Vikings hooded sweat shirt and worn blue jeans.

The man stares at Bedloe, then reaches down to his plate and takes a couple of the remaining fries. He defiantly dips them in Bedloe's ketchup and puts them in his mouth, for some reason challenging the attorney with his rudeness.

"Ain't you that-there lawyer guy out of the Cities tryin' to get the damned child rapist off?"

Bedloe looks up at the intruder, watching him as he munches on his fries, followed by the best Minnesota accent the Chicago native can muster.

"Oh jeez, yah sure you betcha. Y'er dern tootin', by golly, don't cha know."

He then goes back to his normal speech, smiling playfully.

"Sorry, my friend, I just couldn't help myself."

"You ain't no friend'a mine, that's for *damn* sure. I seen what you Twin City shyster lawyers can do to people. You're all nothin' but a bunch'a 'bottom-feedin', low-life money grubbers."

Swain is simmering with anger by all this. He's had about enough and clearly expresses it.

"He's not from the Twin Cities, and my son is innocent. And I've got a question for you.

"Why is it that a dumb northern hillbilly like you can't just keep his stupid *fucking* mouth shut, and mind his own goddamned business?"

Other patrons hear the remark and an agitated murmur is heard throughout the place as the 'fry thief' looks to the table of men he had been sitting with. Angered, he makes a quick aggressive move toward Swain, who responds by standing and kicking his chair out of the way.

Bedloe, shocked at Swain's unaccustomed behavior, looks at the two men facing off, and slowly rises as well.

Swain gives the man a hard, confident stare, along with a smile, and says:

"'Better make the first one count, because that's all you're going to get."

The guy hesitates and looks again to the table of men, and then returns to this solid senior citizen. He loudly announces, as he heavily struts back to his chair, attempting to dismiss the challenge:

"I'll find some woman to do my light work for me, you old bastard."

Swain looks at Bedloe.

"You done?"

"I am now."

Swain reaches into his back pocket and pulls out his wallet. He throws a twenty-dollar bill on the table, more than covering the tab and tip, then says to Bedloe:

"Let's go."

As they leave, an older female voice is heard.

"Go back where ya come from. We don't want yer kind here."

Bedloe leans in toward Swain.

"Well, my friend, what do you think? Have we just been treated to an example of *Minnesota Nice?*"

When they get to the car, Swain informs Bedloe there's still enough time for him to briefly visit with his son's wife, Jean Ballas. He called her the day before and was told that, if possible, to stop by sometime around noon. Bedloe drops him off at his truck. Driving to Ballas' house, Swain calls her from his cell phone to say he's on his way.

Jeremiah Bedloe talked with her earlier in the spring, and was told that she would not testify on her husband's behalf. He asked her the reason, but she wouldn't offer one. Subsequently, the issue was dropped.

When Michael arrives, she is standing on the front porch of the beautiful home that was built by her and her first husband. Her two children from that previous marriage are nowhere in sight. "How are you doing, Jean? It's good to see you again."

"I'm okay."

He moves in closer to her and attempts to complete the greeting with a friendly hug, but sees her flinch and feels a barrier separating them. Nevertheless, she obliges with a stiff, awkward embrace.

Her father-in-law is not invited into the house.

He understands the anger Russell's wife has toward his son, but he also knows how she and the children stood by him after his arrest.


During Michael's initial investigation of the case, Ballas sent him a copy of the letter she had written to the judge presiding over the sentencing hearing. It indicated without reservation, the positive type of husband and father Russell had been, and the surprising negative changes she saw come over him in the year prior to the sexual assault.

The letter said that, after they met in 2007, Russell Swain learned that the children's biological father had abandoned them all years before, so he immediately assumed the parental role, and became totally involved in all their lives.

Russell and Jean married the following year, in the summer of 2008. He then moved from his apartment in St. Paul to Cambridge.

The letter went on to tell the judge that her husband had been a devoted father and step-father. His daughter, Marcianna, was his top priority. In the late fall of 2008, with the assistance of a family therapist, Marcianna pleaded with her father, and his newly blended family, to let her come live with them full-time. When his former wife, Kathryn Trussoni, learned of this, she hired a lawyer and the ensuing custody battle took a heavy toll on Russell and the rest of his family. He, nevertheless, persisted due to his daughter's unrelenting request.

By mid-year, 2009, Jean started to see dramatic psychological changes in Russell's personality. She expressed this to her husband, and he said he was seeking help. However, she had no idea what type of "help" he was seeking. He wouldn't tell her, instead continued to become more and more withdrawn, preferring to be by himself apart from the family. When she asked why he wanted isolation, the response was always:

"I don't know why."

Russell could often be found at night sitting in the darkness of a room, usually in a corner in the basement, alone. His moods were always changing, skipping from mania to depression.

Jean went on to state in the letter:

*"The event that happened on January 2, 2010, I believe was a cry for help. His actions were totally out of character. Within a few days of the incident, he called on our pastor and confessed. What he said that day is unknown to me. All I know is that it takes a remorseful person to tell a man of God of his guilt and struggles."*

Michael and Jean stand outside the picturesque country home on the outskirts of Cambridge. It is a pleasant and cool summer day.

He wants to ask her where the kids are, but again, senses the ongoing barrier separating them. They continue to talk in generalities, and then he gets a jolt when Jean tells him that she and Russell had agreed to divorce.

"When did that happen? Is it final?"

"About three months ago. Yes, we're divorced."

Puzzled and disappointed that his son didn't confide in him, Michael responds.

"I wonder why Russ didn't tell me. How are the kids handling all this?"

"As well as can be expected, I guess."

Michael looks down and then to Jean, shaking his head in sympathy.

"Those kids have been to hell and back too often."

"They'll be okay. My family's there for them."

"That's important. How about you?"

"They're there for me too. I've got my kids, my family, a good job, my health. It could be a hell of a lot worse."

Swain doesn't know whether to stay and talk, or simply say "good-bye" and leave. He wonders why, after two years of battling through all this, they came to the decision to now end the marriage.

"Jean, why? Why now? We're in court. I'm trying my *damnedest* to get Russ the hell out of prison."

An Army veteran and now a sergeant with the St. Paul Police Department, she's not one to mince words. Her face is contorted with pain and resentment.

"Because of that *fucking* ex-wife of his! That's why! She's threatening to take my house and everything she can get her grubby *fucking* hands on, if I don't pay her the money Russ owes for child support and maintenance since he was sent to prison. The fat, ugly *bitch* probably makes well over eighty thousand dollars a year, and she *still* wants to come after *me*.

There's no way in hell she's going get a god-damned dime. No way!"

She adds another reason.

"Get this. I also took out a second mortgage on my home for lawyers' fees, twenty-thousand *fucking* dollars, to fight so Marcianna could come live with us. Do you believe it? So, to be totally honest with you, right about now, I wish to Christ I'd never met your goddamned son."

Jean folds her arms on her chest, and looks up at the sky.

"I apologize. I … I need time. And space from it all. Me and Russ talked it out. It's best for now. As it stands, he's in prison. We'll take it one tick at a time."

He looks at her and forces a smile.

"If it's any consolation, Russ' lawyer destroyed her yesterday."

"I know. It's all over town. And the media. It might be of some consolation to *you* knowing that the minister who turned Russell in was fired and ridden out of town on a rail. Seems he was 'screwing' quite a few of the church women. What a hypocrite. His wife is divorcing him."

Michael shakes his head. "Are you planning at all on being at the trial?"

"No way. I can't handle any more of it. I've got to move on. As for the future, once the kids graduate high school in a few years and go on to college, I'm out of here. Permanently.

This was their father's hometown, not mine. And I'm tired of it. I haven't been able to make a friend.

"And now, because of what Russ did, we're *really* getting shunned and stared at. My kids were also catching hell at school – wise-ass comments and shabby treatment. Not from all the children, but enough of it to make it damn hard on them. I'm glad the trial is going on during summer."

After all is said and done, a good and generous woman, and her children, have been dealt a major blow from this tragedy.

"Jean, I don't know what else to say."

That barrier and her toughness dissolve and she walks over to him. She drapes her arms around his neck, clinging tightly. He can feel her torso heaving in a quiet cry, and his eyes fill with sympathetic emotional tears. After a short spell, they separate and both of them try to smile. Michael Swain looks at her earnestly.

"As God is my witness, I'll try to make it up to you, at least the financial loss. Unfortunately, that's probably all I can do. Say 'Hi' to the kids for me."

"I will. Good luck at the trial."

## Scene Five

# Genetics versus the Law

*The Isanti County courtroom. The same day, 1:30 p.m.*

Bedloe turns to see if Michael Swain has returned. He sees, instead, a deputy sheriff escorting Lorna and Victor Dunn to reserved seats halfway back.

Lorna smiles to her boss and nods, knowing who was responsible for the arrangements. Michael enters and is seated just in time.

"All rise," says the bailiff.

Bedloe turns to face the court.

Judge Guttormsen resumes her position on the bench.

"Please be seated. Deputy, bring the defendant into the courtroom."

The deputy sheriff leaves, and then reenters with Russell Swain, whose shackles, chains, and prison jumpsuit have been removed. He is now dressed in brown cotton trousers, a light blue dress shirt, and a multi-colored brown and blue tie – the same items delivered to the Isanti County Jail by his father to be worn at the trial. The judge looks at Bedloe out of the corner of her eye.

"Mr. Bedloe, call your next witness."

Nodding his approval to the court, he is also thinking, *the power of media.*

"The defense calls Mr. John Morehouse."

Another deputy sheriff leans into the hallway.

*Morehouse is a slender professorial-looking man in his forties, neatly attired in suit and tie. He walks up to the witness stand and is sworn in.*

*Bedloe has been informed by Michael Swain, that John Morehouse has painstakingly supported him and his son from the start. He is one of the leading authorities on 47, XXY-Klinefelter syndrome, and has spent many hours educating this father and son about the spectrum of effects concerning Russell's genetic disorder.*

Jeremiah Bedloe walks to the witness and starts his questioning.

"Sir, you are executive director of an organization called, the *National Association of Klinefelter Syndrome*, or N.A.K.S. Is that correct?"

"Yes."

"How long have you held that title?"

"Since its inception in 2004. I am the founder of N.A.K.S."

228

"Mr. Morehouse, often a person, such as yourself, establishes an organization due to personal reasons, because someone close to them has fallen victim to an illness. Or, in this case, has a genetic disorder.

"Does that apply to you?"

"It does."

"How so?"

"My son has Klinefelter syndrome."

"Is your son 47, XXY, such as the defendant?"

Prosecutor Reese-Hall stands.

"Objection, Your Honor. To my knowledge, it has not been verified in this courtroom that the defendant *has* Klinefelter syndrome."

The judge responds to defense counsel for verification.

"Mr. Bedloe?"

"Your Honor, the post-conviction relief petition clearly states that, in 1996, my client was diagnosed with Klinefelter syndrome by Dr. Anthony Reinquist, then an endocrinologist at the Gundersen Clinic in La Crosse, Wisconsin. He is now at the Mayo Clinic in Rochester, Minnesota. I will gladly provide the prosecution with this verification immediately after today's session, if you so rule."

Judge Guttormsen glances briefly at Reese-Hall, and then goes back to Bedloe.

"That will not be necessary. I'll examine the petition myself. Continue, counsel."

Bedloe returns to the witness.

"Mr. Morehouse, my previous question concerned your son's condition."

"My son is 48, XXYY."

"What is the difference between your son and Mr. Swain?"

"There are numerous variations of Klinefelter syndrome, according to the karyotype the male was born with."

"Karyotype?"

"The chromosomal organizational number each human has. The *normal* karyotype for the male is 46, XY, twenty-three coming from the mother, twenty-three from the father. By genetic accident, Mr. Swain was born with one additional X chromosome, therefore he's 47, XXY. My son is 48, XXYY, in other words, he has one additional X chromosome, and an addition Y chromosome as well."

"Why are these differences significant?"

Morehouse folds his arms on his chest.

"The different karyotypes predominantly result in the degree of affect each variant has on the male. Some people are hardly affected at all, while others are profoundly affected. The karyotype and degree of affect can manifest itself into symptoms from a panoply of comorbid psychological conditions. This can range from mental health issues, a significant immaturity from executive functioning problems, to ADHD and autism spectrum disorders."

"And your son?"

The father's arms slowing drop, then folds his hands on his lap.

"Being 48, XXYY, my son, who is fourteen-years-old now, is affected to the extent he cannot function in many of the ways a 46, XY male can. He must attend schools that specifically deal in special education and special needs, and must be monitored in terms of personal hygiene and nutrition. Later in life, there is a high degree of probability he will not be able to attend college or hold a job. For all intents and purposes, and to make a long story short, he … will be profoundly challenged for his entire life."

"Mr. Morehouse, I do not want to appear flippant, but to the average lay-person such as myself, it would seem inconceivable that the mere existence of an extra chromosome or two could have that much effect."

Morehouse smiles, sadly.

"Believe me, sir, it does."

"And what about the male who is 47, XXY? What is the prognosis for him?"

"Usually much better. The difficulties frequently involve learning disabilities, emotional and mental developmental issues, and decision-making capabilities. The 47, XXY male struggles with, among other things, cognitive deficits, impulse control disorders, and executive functioning problems.

Seldom is the 47, XXY male challenged to the extent the 48, XXYY male is."

"Would you briefly explain to the jury, cognitive deficits, impulse control, and executive functioning as they apply to the 47, XXY adult male?"

"Briefly?" Morehouse smiles. "I'll try."

He then faces the jury, and again fold his arms across his chest.

"First of all, the term *cognitive deficits* refers to characteristics that act as a barrier to cognition, the thinking process. It can range from mental retardation, at one extreme, to learning disabilities, dyslexia, or reading comprehension problems, on the other. Most 47, XXY males are dyslexic.

"*Impulse control disorder* in the 47, XXY male usually occurs when he is being subjected to extreme, prolonged stress. While stressed, he feels unable to resist acting on urges to do something, even behaviors that could end up harming him or another person or persons. It's important to state that these behaviors are not planned. They're impulsive. Interestingly, the behaviors bring some relief from the stress, but then he often realizes how out of proportion his actions were, resulting in oppressive guilt and remorse."

"And, lastly, Mr. Morehouse, *executive functioning*?"

"It is consistently associated with Attention Deficit Hyperactivity Disorder, or ADHD."

"Sir, pardon the interruption," Bedloe says, facing the jury. "It should be stated here that the MidState Medical Center diagnosed my client with ADHD in 2008, and that is a matter of record. Please proceed, Mr. Morehouse."

"Certainly. Mainly, the 47, XXY male with *executive functioning* problems has difficulty controlling emotions, he tends to act or speak before thinking, not using 'self-talk' to control behavior or future actions."

Morehouse shifts in the witness chair, and then continues.

"Also, he will very often exhibit extreme immaturity and have the emotional development of someone well behind his chronological age. This immaturity continues in varying degrees throughout adolescence and into adulthood, and will also vary in intensity with each individual 47, XXY male."

Bedloe turns from the jury and stares first at John Morehouse, and then at his client. It feels as if a bolt of lightning has just passed through his body. His mind begins to race, and he can't focus on the witness. He is instead overwhelmed with a disturbing thought.

He falls silent, attempting to drive it from his mind so he can continue concentration on the trial, but it persists. He instantly goes from Russell Swain, then back to John Morehouse and his last response about immaturity.

Bedloe walks over to the bench.

"Your Honor, the defense has an unorthodox request, a one-hour recess in order to have a private meeting with the defendant, the witness, and myself. I would also request that the defendant's father, Michael Swain, be allowed to join us."

233

Judge Guttormsen looks at the prosecutor.

"Ms. Reese-Hall?"

She impatiently shakes her head. "No objection."

"Very well. The deputy will show you all to the private room across the hall. The court is in recess for exactly one hour, no longer."


The four men sit at a large table in the room. The deputy sheriff is just outside the door. Bedloe looks at Morehouse.

"John, this immaturity thing, is it across the board? I mean, does it manifest itself in adults, whereby the 47, XXY male makes emotional decisions in life in a way similar to what younger people do?"

"Yes. From a brain developmental standpoint, they can be, in some ways, cognitively and emotionally similar. Why do you ask?"

Bedloe doesn't respond, but looks at Russell Swain for the longest time. As nuts as it may appear to the others, he asks his client the question that's been gnawing at his mind.

"Being Marcianna's father, I know you love your daughter. I know that. What's troubling the hell out of me is, do you feel that you, for God's sake, are you in love with this girl?"

Russell immediately drops his head. Morehouse looks at Bedloe, then to Michael Swain, whose thoughts are now entirely on Jean Ballas and her two children.

Morehouse responds. "Jeremiah, 47, XXY men often prefer the company of much younger people, however ..."

"Yeah, but do they fall in *love* with them?"

"I suppose it could happen in their mind but really, that appears to be a stretch."

Bedloe speaks to his client.

"Russell, on second thought, the three of us are going to talk about this, and ask that you leave. Your dad and I will discuss it with you later. Don't concern yourself with it, it may not even be relevant. I need to know what we're dealing with here. It has nothing to do with the trial."

In fact, it has a lot to do with the trial, and the attorney knows that.

Bedloe summons the deputy and then goes to his client, who impatiently looks to the ceiling, clearly indicating he wants all this to be over with. The attorney pats his shoulder.

Russell stands, still looking upward, and he seems confused. Michael gives his son a sustained, emotional hug. It is now evident to him, John, and even Jeremiah, that Russ' Klinefelter syndrome mind is – God only knows where.

The defendant leaves the room, and Bedloe looks to everyone remaining.

He walks around the table, rubbing the back of his neck.

"What if Russell feels that he is in love with this girl? She's not his biological daughter. And he's got to be what, thirty-years older than she is. Yet, there was something he said during our meeting at Moose Lake that troubled me. He became very emotional and blurted out: 'Mr. Bedloe, you can't call Marcianna as a witness.

*"I love her.'*

"It stuck with me for some reason, just the way he said it.

"John, Michael, help me out here. Is this really too far-fetched?"

Morehouse looks at Swain while hesitantly addressing Bedloe, still doubting the premise.

"Klinefelter syndrome or 'KS' guys have a tendency to misread social cues from others, and have a hard time identifying emotions like anger or fear, but this ..."

Swain's mind returns to the issue at hand.

"Maybe even love and sexual cues as well? Hell, even some kind of *Lolita Complex*."

Morehouse shakes his head. "Believe me, I know a tad about classic fiction, and this whole thing has nothing to do with Nabokov's novel, *Lolita*.

"However, some recent court cases have involved adult KS males who sexually assaulted young girls. So, it's not 'far-fetched' that a girl sitting on their lap, or a hug, even a smile, could be misinterpreted by them as romantic or sexual, as opposed to child-adult affection. These guys can also be self-centered in their approach, seeking their own gratification through bonding. So, which way is it?"

Swain nods and then responds to Morehouse's evaluation, recalling his son's childhood.

"I remember Russ always being very selfish. It's normal for a kid to be egocentric, but that gives way to sharing and empathy as they grow into adolescence and beyond. It's very Freudian, but I believe it."

He hesitates, and then continues.

"With my son, it never happened. He didn't develop. In reading Dr. Lagerfeldt's report, he felt that Russ had symptoms of what he called a *narcissistic personality disorder.*"

He looks at Morehouse. "Maybe the extreme egocentrism due to Klinefelter became fixated in adolescence and developed into narcissism?"

Morehouse again shakes his head, continuing the dialogue.

"I don't think it is *fixation or narcissism,* but just how these guys think. The KS adult male could very well simply misread or misunderstand the child sitting on his lap as sexual love, even though the child looks at it merely as sharing affection."

Morehouse is unaware of earlier prosecution testimony suggesting sexual participation by Russell's daughter.

He goes on. "It's absolutely imperative to remember, the KS mind perceives the world differently than we do. Maybe his daughter is now viewed by him as a girlfriend, *especially* since she's not his biological daughter."

He turns to Swain.

"Michael, is the girl aware of this fact?"

"Yes. She was told at around eight years of age."

Morehouse completes his point.

"So, again, the question seems to be, are these cognitive distortions on a conscious level normal to him as a middle-aged KS adult? Or was it for self-serving, egocentric reasons? Did he know what he did and why?"

Swain somewhat changes the subject. Bedloe remains silent, preferring to listen and maybe learn something.

"Along with all this, I've read about other emotional responses so often found in 47, XXY males when they're kids. In childhood, Russ would act irrationally and inappropriately to other people and to himself. He also had so many fears and phobias, insecurities, sensitivities, apprehensions, and often cried at the slightest thing.

"He also had God-awful problems with kids in the neighborhood and at school, being bullied and made fun of – he just wouldn't fight back.

"Maybe he gravitates towards younger people now, who he feels more comfortable with and can be in control of because he's bigger and older?"

Morehouse then says:

"There's a term we use called, *emotional congruence*, which refers to an adult's emotional needs and a child's personality traits within him. For example, if the KS adult's self-perception *is* child-like, he may wish to relate to younger people on their level, and feel more comfortable doing so.

Despite Michael Swain's profound respect for John Morehouse, all this "psycho-babble" is starting to irritate him, including his own.

He stands and looks at Morehouse. "Let's cut to the chase here. I've read over and over again in the research, that Klinefelter syndrome can result in mental retardation. John, you've told me in the past that people in N.A.K.S. don't want to hear that, and push back hard at the mention of it. But personally, at times in my son's life, I thought he had retardation but then I couldn't imagine why. Now I can.

"This one little goddamned extra chromosome is certain to be responsible for behaviors that end up impairing Russell's ability to think straight like a normal 46, XY adult man. Okay, I get it. He has a hard time controlling emotions, he acts before he thinks, and immature as hell, along with other things.

*"Then*, add to this the drugs that were fed to him? My God, when you think of the condition he must've been in, the results could've been even worse than what he did that day.

"Before this disaster blew up two years ago, it never crossed my mind that he was having thoughts about my granddaughter, and now there's the possibility he's *in love* with her? What the hell is going on in that man's mind? As long as I'm alive, they will reunite as father and daughter, and stay that way. There will be nothing else.

"How can any rational, intelligent human being seriously ignore my son's need for specialists who deal in all these issues? Only when they're in his life, will he know what has to be done, so that he can have some kind of successful future.

"And there's no doubt in my mind, that when you look at what little help he's gotten for the last two years, it's next to *impossible* for anything to become reality while in that prison system.

"That's why I want him out!"


*The trial resumes. Jeremiah Bedloe moves into an entirely different area of examination with John Morehouse. Yet, it is ultimately for the same purpose, to present a complete picture of his client.*

*Bedloe feels as though he has come to know Russell and Michael Swain as well as he's known anyone else in his life.*

*He is reinvigorated, and ready to proceed aggressively against the state of Minnesota's effort to keep his client in prison.*


"Now, Mr. Morehouse, I'd like to move into a more specific area concerning Klinefelter syndrome – the testosterone given to Russell Swain by the MidState Medical Center during the latter part of 2009.

"On May 14, 2011, you wrote a letter to the Isanti County Judicial District Court, and it was written at the request of Russell's father, Michael Swain. Is that right?"

"Yes."

"Did you bring a copy of it with you?

"I did."

Bedloe addresses the judge.

"This communication is a matter of record, and it was also included in the post-conviction relief petition."

He returns to Morehouse.

"The letter was written after Michael Swain provided you with his son's prescribed dosages of injected testosterone, and the resulting blood testosterone levels during the last months of 2009, as shown in Russell's records from the MidState Medical Center. Correct?"

"Yes, that is correct."

Bedloe again addresses the judge.

"The county has a copy of this medical record as well."

He goes back to the witness.

"Sir, what was the purpose of your letter?"

"To show the changes in the prescribed dosages of testosterone given to Russell by the medical center during its androgen replacement therapy program, and the possible ramifications."

"Would you please explain, androgen replacement therapy?"

Morehouse responds.

"When a Klinefelter syndrome male enters puberty, and then grows into adulthood, it is imperative he be given regular doses of testosterone in order to replace the androgen missing due to this chromosomal disorder. It is important to the emotional and physical wellbeing of the male, that he be given the proper dose."

"So, once you reviewed his specific testosterone dosages and blood levels, as shown in Russell's records from the medical center, what was found?"

"The medical record showed that his ongoing injected testosterone was changed to Androgel, a topically applied medication, on November 23, 2009."

"Mr. Morehouse, you are aware the sexual assault occurred on January 2, 2010, are you not?"

"That's my understanding. According to a consultant on our staff who specializes in testosterone replacement therapies, and an adult 47, XXY male himself, this five-week period was enough time for radical shifts in testosterone levels to be fully manifested in Mr. Swain's emotions and behaviors."

"How did your consultant determine that?"

"He related that Mr. Swain's medical record showed important facts.  First, while receiving testosterone by injection, his dose was high and his blood levels were increasing.  His last test while receiving injections showed that his dose was too high.

"Then, when changed to Androgel, his one and only blood test showed the blood testosterone levels had dropped precipitously, which *very* often results in a severely emotional roller-coaster ride.

"But for some reason he was abruptly changed back to the injections."

"Sir, please read to the jury the second to the last paragraph of your letter to the district court."

Morehouse proceeds.

*"The emotional distress associated with poor testosterone management, combined with well-known developmental issues related to 47, XXY, were likely contributors to Russell Swain's behaviors and should serve as mitigating factors when assessing his culpability."*

"Mr. Morehouse.  One more question.  We have mentioned various names for the substance medically given for a prolonged period to Mr. Swain; namely, androgen, testosterone, and hormone.  Isn't there another name for them, one usually associated with athletes?"

"Yes."

"Please inform the jury what that is."

"Anabolic steroid."

Bedloe looks to the jury, and then to prosecutor Reese-Hall.

"Your witness."

He quickly states to Judge Guttormsen: "Subject to redirect, Your Honor."

Reese-Hall aggressively walks to stand in front of Morehouse.


"Mr. Morehouse, please inform the jury what your last level of education is."

"I have a master's degree."

"In what subject area?"

"English Literature."

"Is that the extent of your education?"

"It is."

"Besides being executive director of the Klinefelter organization, do you have full-time employment?"

"Yes and no. I am an adjunct professor in literature at the University of Colorado at Boulder, which is three-quarters of a full-time contract."

"So, you have no background in medicine? You are not a doctor?

"No, I am not."

"Pharmacist?"

"No."

"I think you know where I'm going with this, right?"

John Morehouse does not respond. Reese-Hall goes to stand facing the jury.

"Further, you mentioned a consultant on your staff with, as you called it, a *specialty* in androgen replacement therapy. Would you name him please?"

"Zelbert Wilder."

"Is Mr. Wilder a medical doctor, pharmacist or chemist?"

"No."

Reese-Hall returns to the witness, seemingly to plead with him for understanding.

"Mr. Morehouse, defense counsel is stating that Russell Swain should not be held responsible for raping his daughter, using *diminished capacity* as a defense, and this was due to a change in his hormone dosage. *And,* it appears the determination as to its effect, if there was any, is being made by two gentlemen not qualified to do so.  Do you agree?"

Bedloe stands.  "I object, Your Honor.  The defense has not yet called further witnesses.  We are not suggesting a hormone alone is responsible for the sexual assault."

"Mr. Bedloe, your objection is overruled.  The prosecution makes a valid point, and will be allowed to proceed with her line of cross-examination."

Bedloe continues to appear upset by the judge's rulings, and realizes nothing will change that.  However, he also knows the jury is hearing it all.

The prosecutor goes back to the witness.

"Mr. Morehouse, do you agree that you two men are not qualified to judge the drug's negative effects?"

"If college degrees are the only relevant criteria, then I'd have to answer 'yes.'"

Bedloe again challenges, this time as aggressively as Reese-Hall.

"I object.  Granted, Mr. Morehouse and Mr. Wilder are not doctors, nor pharmacists, or for that matter, chemists.  The testimony here, or written deposition presented, is for the sole purpose of offering a summary of the accumulated knowledge from those endocrinologists specializing in sex chromosomal disorders who, in turn, then provide it to N.A.K.S.  The mission of this organization is to use that knowledge in order to assist males with this disorder, and their families, by forwarding *information* to them, not treatment."

The prosecutor comes back as assertively.

"I am simply attempting to enter into the record whether or not these witnesses' testimonies and depositions as presented, are laymen's positions taken or have been professionally determined."

The judge looks at Bedloe to respond.

"Your Honor, the defense has already conceded that Mr. Morehouse and Mr. Wilder are not medical professionals. The defense is asking the court to recognize that these two men have extremely vast knowledge of the administration of testosterone and the affects that can occur if the male is given the incorrect dosage."

"Mr. Bedloe," Judge Guttormsen says, "the court will temporarily overrule your objection, allowing the prosecutor's questioning. If the defense is going to present testimony that supports its case, the prosecution should be allowed to challenge it and then let the jury decide its value. Continue, carefully, Madam Prosecutor."

"I have no more questions for the witness. Enough time has been wasted on all this. We learned enough."

Bedloe asks the witness on re-direct.

"Mr. Morehouse, let's 'waste' a little more time, shall we? Please give the jury a brief list of sex chromosomal disorders other than Kline …"

Guttormsen interrupts.

"Mr. Morehouse, before you answer, please relate to the court what significance there is, if any, of knowing what other sicknesses there are besides this Klinefelter thing.  As the prosecutor stated, perhaps we are wasting time with all this here."

Bedloe is aghast at the judge for interrupting him and addressing his witness.

"This is my witness, Your Honor, not yours.  If you wish to take over the defense, let me know and I'll run into the Cities to catch a Twins game."  There is laughter in the courtroom.

"Mr. Bedloe, this court has every right to speak to the witness."

Then the judge wearily addresses the jury.

"Ladies and gentlemen, we are in recess for one-half hour.  Mr. Bedloe, you will again meet me in my chambers."

"All rise."


The two are in the judge's chambers.  Bedloe is the first to speak.

"I don't wish to say anything to you without a witness present."

Judge Guttormsen walks back into the courtroom, gesturing for the bailiff to join them.  She sits while Bedloe remains standing.

"Mr. Bedloe, I've recently learned of the brushes you've had with censuring and near disbarments, both in Minnesota and Wisconsin. You're no stranger to that thing. So, I'll keep your record alive and well, if you do not stop your contemptuous public behavior, especially for all the media to see and hear!"

Bedloe slams his fist hard against the judge's desk. The bailiff jumps.

"You know a lot about my judicial record? Then perhaps you also know of the influences I have in this state. I'll move a mountain to get you impeached if you interfere with my examination of a witness with your prejudicial conduct! By the way, I don't give a gopher's ass about the parasite media, and neither should you!"

The bailiff's face is red. Bedloe continues.

"And I heard about you as well. You couldn't cut it as a lawyer in the private sector, even in Stillwater. The outcome of this trial will depend on me, the prosecutor, and the jury."

Both Bedloe and Guttormsen are furious, but with the bailiff present, the judge struggles to control her temper and points a shaking finger to the door.

"Counsel, we're going back into that courtroom. You run your case in a professional manner now, and ask the witnesses what you have to. But keep it relevant and to the point. I want no more lollygagging here. Do you understand?"

"I understand. I certainly understand."

*The recess is concluded. The judge is seated and John Morehouse is back on the stand.*

Jeremiah Bedloe continues with his witness.

"Mr. Morehouse, you were asked to relate any sex chromosomal disorders other than Klinefelter syndrome. Please give the jury a brief list."

"Certainly. As I previously mentioned, these genetic disorders are due to abnormal variations in chromosomal counts, and include not only XXYY, XXY Klinefelter, and XYY syndromes in males, but also singular X or Turner syndrome and Triple X syndrome in females, along with Trisomy 18 or Edwards syndrome being eighty percent female. Lastly, there is the well-known Down syndrome, or Trisomy 21, in both sexes."

"Sir, along with physical disabilities associated with each, are there secondary psychological disorders as well?"

"Yes."

"From memory, please name some of them."

"Common ones often found are attention deficit, autism spectrum, dyslexia, and depression, just to name a few. Studies have also included bipolar affective disorder, schizophrenia, and mental retardation, probably most noticeable in Down syndrome."

Bedloe looks at Reese-Hall.

"So, as the prosecutor suggested, perhaps our society should stop wasting time on all these people."

She jumps to her feet.

"I object, your Honor.  That statement is insulting and insensitive!"

"Objection sustained."

Bedloe stays on task and continues.  "The jury is asked to recall that Dr. Paul Lagerfeldt suggested symptoms of bipolar affective disorder and schizoaffective disorder in his findings concerning Mr. Swain, but he has never been medically diagnosed with either.   However, he has been diagnosed with attention deficit disorder and severe depression.  We will return to this point shortly."

Bedloe moves on to another subject.

"Mr. Morehouse, your association has maintained a steadily increasing data base of endocrinologists in the United States who specialize in Klinefelter syndrome.  Is that right?"

"Yes."

"How many do specialize in this genetic disorder?"

"As far we know, fourteen.  And they deal predominately with children and adolescents."

"How many are in the state of Minnesota?"

"According to our data base, one, at the Mayo Clinic in Rochester, Minnesota."

"Does your organization know how many males in this country have Klinefelter syndrome?"

"It's commonly known that the number is one out every five hundred to eight hundred males, world-wide."

Bedloe continues.

"I was already aware of that.  The male population in the United States is about one hundred and forty million.  As a result, that's approximately 175,000 to 280,000 males with Klinefelter syndrome at any given time.

"Sir, with that large of a number, where does information and support come from to help the males and their families who unfortunately do not have a specialist nearby?"

"From our organization, and others around the country."

"When physicians, other than endocrinologists, need knowledge or recommendations in order to assist with Klinefelter patients, where does that information come from?"

"Again, often from our organization and other satellite organizations in this country and around the world. Unfortunately, we're just now starting to understand the vast number of issues these men and boys are dealing with."

"Does your organization know how many 47, XXY males are *adults*?"

"No, it's probably around half.  A significant number of adult males have not been medically diagnosed because their disorder is mild.  If they find out later in life, it's usually due to a sterility test to determine why they cannot impregnate a woman.

"Also, if a man has been diagnosed later in life, it's often due to troubles in their personal and work relationships, or legal issues like bankruptcy or incarceration."

"How many endocrinologists specialize in treating those adult males who have been diagnosed with 47, XXY later in life?"

"To our knowledge, two."

"How many specialists are there in the state of Minnesota?"

"According to our data base, none."

"Last question.  What are the chances Russell Swain would receive treatment for 47, XXY if he remains in prison and is therefore unable to leave the state of Minnesota?"

"Virtually zero chance."

"Thank you, Mr. Morehouse.  No further questions."

The judge speaks to the witness.  "You are excused, Mr. Morehouse.  The court thanks you for your testimony.  Mr. Bedloe, call your next witness."

"Your Honor, the defense would like to move into the area of doctors who prescribed medications to my client in late 2008, and all of 2009."

253

Judge Guttormsen anxiously looks at her watch. "How long will this take?"

He looks at his watch. "At the latest, a few minutes after four."

The judge stares at the back entrance to the courtroom.

"Then … proceed then."

## Scene Six

# The MidState Medical Center

*Three physicians from the MidState Medical Center who prescribed medications for Russell Swain were subpoenaed to testify, and were ordered by the court to produce documents and records at the trial.*

*All three doctors are in the hallway, waiting to be called.*

"The defense calls Dr. Judith Pruitt as the next witness."

Dr. Pruitt enters the courtroom and is sworn in. Bedloe picks up a copy of her records and reports concerning Russell Swain, and puts on his reading glasses. He then walks to the witness.

"My examination of you, doctor, will be brief," he says. "You are a staff psychiatrist at the MidState Medical Center, is that correct?"

"It is."

"You were subpoenaed to appear at this trial, accompanied by records and reports concerning my client, Russell Howard Swain. Did you bring them with you today?"

"I did."

"Good. On October 22, 2008, Mr. Swain arrived for his first appointment with you. Correct?"

"Yes."

"Upon completion of that first appointment, did you diagnosis him with ADHD and suggest a trial of the medication Adderall XR, twenty milligrams daily?"

"Yes."

"Three months later, on January 29, 2009, did you diagnose Mr. Swain with severe depression, and prescribe to him a daily dosage of citalopram, twenty milligrams?"

"That is correct."

"Then, upon prescribing these two serious medications, from January 29 until July 10, 2009, *a six-month period,* the medical records show no doctor-patient interaction of any kind between you and the defendant. *And*, the *July* appointment was with Dr. Thomas Baumgartner, another staff psychiatrist at the medical center.

"For that entire period of time, there is no record or report of Mr. Swain being your patient, or anyone else's for that matter. Was he your patient, or was he Dr. Baumgartner's during that six months?"

"I certainly do not recall the answer to that question."

"Doctor, when you first prescribed Adderall and citalopram, did you inform Mr. Swain of possible side-effects involved with each drug?"

"Yes, I did."

"Are you certain of that?"

"Yes.  It's common procedure."

"Do you know if Mr. Swain was taking Adderall and citalopram during that six-month period?"

"I do not."

"Were you aware that the defendant was receiving bi-monthly injections of an *anabolic steroid* during the time you prescribed both medications?"

Dr.  Pruitt hesitates.

"Doctor?"

"No ... I don't recall."

"Your Honor, I have no further questions."

Judge Guttormsen speaks.

"Ms. Reese-Hall, cross-examination?"

"No, Your Honor."

"Dr. Pruitt, you are excused.  The court appreciates your appearing at this trial."

Bedloe says,

"The defense calls Dr. Thomas Baumgartner."

He walks back to his table to pick up another report.

When Pruitt leaves the stand, she meets Baumgartner in the courtroom's center aisle, but they don't look at one another or speak.

Baumgartner takes the stand and is sworn in. Bedloe then walks to the witness.

"Dr. Baumgartner, you're also a staff psychiatrist at the MidState Medical Center, is that correct?"

"Yes, I am."

"During the entire year of 2009?"

"Yes."

"You were subpoenaed to appear at this trial, and bring your complete medical records and reports concerning Russell Howard Swain. Are they with you today?"

"They are."

"Thank you. From those records and reports, please relate to the jury and the court, any medications you prescribed for Mr. Swain during the year 2009."

"According to my records, I recommended he switch from his ongoing Adderall prescription to Vyvanse."

"What was the initial dosage of Vyvanse you prescribed?"

"Thirty milligrams daily."

"Was this solely your recommendation?"

"No. Janice Nelson, Mr. Swain's psychologist, stated she felt he had what Dr. Daniel Amen referred to in his book on

ADHD as the #6 Ring of Fire, and co-recommended the Vyvanse.  In the book ..."

"Excuse me doctor, it's not necessary to delve into Dr. Amen's book at this time.  More important are the medications. Did you increase the dosage of Vyvanse?"

"I did."

"To what?"

"To seventy milligrams daily."

"Was that a maximum dosage?"

"For all intents and purposes, it was."

"Dr. Baumgartner, was it or wasn't it?"

"Yes ... it was."

"Thank you.  Why was the dosage increased?"

"According to my records, it was due to extreme depression resulting from stresses Mr. Swain was enduring in his life during that period in time."

"Do you have the date this maximum dosage was prescribed?"

"Yes, it was on October the sixteenth, 2009."

"Did you inform Mr. Swain of the side-effects associated with this medication, and especially the maximum dosage?"

"Yes."

"Moving on. Did you prescribe diazepam to the defendant during this same time?"

"Yes, I did."

"The date, please."

Dr. Baumgartner looks for the date in his records.

"On December the eleventh, 2009."

"Why was he prescribed this medication?"

"Mr. Swain informed me he has a severe fear of flying, in commercial airlines, that is. Diazepam is a mild sedative, a.k.a. Valium, and is often used by patients to reduce anxiety, including flying."

"You mentioned the term *mild.* How mild?"

"Medications are often put on a schedule of one through five, 'one' being *very powerful*, and 'five' being *very mild.* Diazepam is a schedule four medication."

"Are there any side-effects associated with diazepam?"

"Very few, if taken as directed, of course."

"One last question. Were you aware of any other medications prescribed for Mr. Swain at that time, by other doctors at the medical center, including injections of an anabolic steroid?"

Dr. Baumgartner again looks through both his records and reports for some time, and then states:

"I don't seem to have that information with me."

"Thank you, doctor.  No further questions."

Judge Guttormsen speaks.  "Prosecution, cross-examine?"

No, Your Honor."  The judge does not look at the witness.

"Dr. Baumgartner, you are excused.  Thank you for appearing.  Mr. Bedloe, call your next witness."

"The defense calls Dr. Rebecca Harold."

Again, Bedloe walks back to his table, drops one report, and picks up another.  He waits for the witness.

Drs. Baumgartner and Harold pass in the center aisle, where they both nod and smile politely to each other. Harold is sworn in.  She appears to be very nervous and anxious. Bedloe immediately picks up on it.


"Dr. Harold, this won't take long.  What is your specialty at the MidState Medical Center?"

"Sleep disorders."

"Do you recall Russell Howard Swain being a patient of yours in 2009?"  She looks at the defendant.

"I do now.  I've had a lot of patients since 2009.  He has lost considerable weight."

"Yes, yes he has.  Prison tends to have that effect on someone.

"Doctor, as was the case with the two previous physicians who testified, you were subpoenaed to appear at this trial with records and reports concerning Mr. Swain. Is that what you're holding?"

"Yes, sir. It is."

"All right. Give the date you first met with Mr. Swain."

She looks at the first page of her report.

"October 15, 2009."

"On that date, was he diagnosed with a medical condition?"

"I diagnosed Mr. Swain with severe obstructive sleep apnea."

"Along with this diagnosis, was a medication prescribed?"

"Yes."

"What was it?"

"I prescribed ten milligrams of Ambien in pill form, to be taken nightly, twenty minutes before bed."

"For what reason?"

"Patients with sleep apnea often have difficulty tolerating the needed devise used while sleeping, and have trouble getting to sleep because of it. The medication was to aid in this process."

"How many Ambien pills were prescribed for him?"

She looks through her papers.

"A year's supply."

"Given such a large supply of this powerful medication, would it be conceivable that a patient, having continued difficulty sleeping, might take more than one-ten-milligram Ambien tablet on a given night?"

"Yes, of course it's conceivable. A physician cannot control the private behaviors of patients."

"Was the defendant informed of the serious side-effects often associated with Ambien?"

"Yes. My nurse informs patients of that."

Bedloe smiles and then walks closer to Harold and stops, putting one hand on the witness stand railing.

"Lastly, during the year 2009, were you aware of any other medications simultaneously prescribed for Mr. Swain by the medical center's physicians other than yourself, including anabolic steroid injections?"

The doctor becomes upset.

"I … I believe it would be best to consult with my attorney before answering that question."

"That is clearly your right, doctor."

He could've pressed the issue but instead turns to face the judge.

"Your Honor, I have no further questions for this subpoenaed witness. Subject to recall."

"Very well.  Madam Prosecutor?"

"No, Your Honor."

"Dr. Harold, you are excused. Thank you."

Dr. Harold walks out of the courtroom with her head down, holding the records and reports tightly to her chest.  The judge says,

"This Court is adjourned until nine a.m. tomorrow morning."

"All rise."


Preferring not to return to the same restaurant for dinner, Bedloe and Michael Swain get in Bedloe's rental car to find somewhere else to eat.  They cruise the main city street filled with private businesses, which is also Highway 95.  As they reach the town limits on the west side, and finding nothing of interest, Bedloe makes an illegal U-turn and heads back in an easterly direction.  After a moment, a brief siren blast is heard behind them.  Swain turns around in the passenger seat, and Bedloe looks in his rearview mirror. Both men see a sheriff's patrol car with its amber and blue lights flashing.  Bedloe reacts.

"Aw, damn it."

He pulls over and rolls down his window.  The sheriff's deputy turns off the lights, gets out of his car, and walks to the driver's side.

"Good afternoon, officer."

"Afternoon, Mr. Bedloe."

Bedloe and Swain look at each other, anticipating another confrontation.

"I'll betcha have no idea why I pulled you over."

Bedloe asks the obvious question in response.

"Might it have something to do with that U-turn?"

"No sir, although you did break the law there."

He and the deputy momentarily look at each other, wondering who should speak next. The deputy starts.

"I was off-duty this noontime and was in the restaurant you two were in for lunch. Just wanted you to know that not all of us in these parts act like that moron did. He was probably half-drunk, as usual."

To which Bedloe responds with playful criticism:

"I can see where that wouldn't be all that hard to do. There seem to be quite a few bars and liquor stores in this town."

The deputy smiles. "'Noticed that, did you?" He then bends down and looks at the passenger.

"Mr. Swain?"

Michael nods.

"I was one of the deputies who arrested your son. I was also on duty in the courtroom durin' his sentencing hearing. Seemed like an okay guy, who did a rotten thing. Off the record, that prosecutor's gone now. She definitely had an anger problem and took it out in the courtroom."

He goes on.

"Everyone in town, includin' me, knew what was gonna happen to your son, especially knowin' who the judge and prosecutor were – as far as treatment and sentences go. Well, anyway, in most cases, strangers don't get no breaks around here."

The deputy sheriff goes back to Bedloe.

"You're causin' quite a stir, Mr. Bedloe. It's all over town about your quittin' the case and tellin' those women they're against men and all."

He gives out with a macho laugh, indicating he doesn't disagree with the assessment. The young deputy then nods, and tells them they're free to go. Bedloe replies.

"Thank you, deputy. I got to ask something before we do. When you 'hit' the siren, how'd you know it was me? It's a rental car."

The deputy smiles. "Trade secret. Oh, one more thing. Don't know if you've been watchin' the TV, but you're becomin' pretty famous. And folks around here don't much like the attention, especially from the Cities. Take my advice, best you both have your meals and lodgin' in North Branch instead of here. The two towns hate each other, so you should be welcomed there with open arms. Have a good rest of the day now."

The lawyer in Bedloe can't let it go.

"Thanks for the advice, but I've just got to ask one more question.  How'd you know we've got rooms in Cambridge?"

The deputy turns to leave.

"It's a small town.  Drive safe now.  Good luck in court tomorrow."

As they drive off, Bedloe turns to Michael and laughs.

"Well, that was a rush.  How about going to North Branch for dinner, then make room reservations starting tomorrow?"

"Sounds like a plan."

After a moment, Swain says,

"Jeremiah, I'll bet you the dinner tab, we just met the author of the note left in your car door."

## Scene Seven

# A Drug Cocktail

*Thursday, nine a.m.*

"All rise."

Judge Guttormsen sits down.

"Mr. Bedloe, call your next witness."

"The defense calls Pamela Arneson."

She walks into the courtroom and is sworn in.

*The witness is late forties or early fifties, with partially gray shoulder-length hair. Dressed in a brown pants suit, she wears an abundance of silver and turquoise Southwestern Native American jewelry on her wrists, fingers, neck, and ears.*

*An athletic physique and androgynous mannerisms, along with a slightly weathered face, suggests she is active in her native Colorado's Rocky Mountain activities.*

Bedloe starts the examination while standing behind his table.

"Ms. Arneson, what is your occupation?"

"Mr. Bedloe, I would prefer being called 'Mrs.', if you don't mind. I am married."

He acknowledges the request, and she answers the question.

"I am a pharmacist."

"Where are you employed?"

"At the Parkview Health Center in Pueblo, Colorado."

"How long have you been employed there?"

"Eighteen years."

"What is your last level of education?"

"I have a master's degree in pharmaceutical science from the University of Colorado at Denver, and I'm presently working on my doctorate."

"Mrs. Arneson, you were not subpoenaed to appear as a witness, but rather, you volunteered. How is it that a pharmacist from Colorado agreed to do that?"

The witness looks at Michael Swain and smiles. Bedloe moves closer as she responds.

"Russell Swain's father and I have been communicating, mostly by internet mail, for quite some time. Through our correspondences, I have come to know quite a lot about his son. We both belong to the National Association of Klinefelter Syndrome and use their chat room."

"Then, you share something in common?"

"Yes. My late son had Klinefelter syndrome."

"How old was your son when he died, and how did he die?"

"Justin was sixteen. He was murdered by two bullies older than him."

Bedloe stands near her. "For purposes of the trial, it's not necessary to delve into this tragic family event, except to say I am truly sorry to hear of your loss.

"Ma'am, with the defendant's approval, Michael Swain sent you a copy of his son's complete medical records and reports from the MidState Medical Center, which specifically included the medications prescribed during the year 2009. Correct?"

"Yes."

"In your professional opinion then, what was your conclusion once the review of all this material was completed?"

"There is a significant possibility that, during the year 2009, Russell Swain was poly pharmaceutically medicated, possibly even to the extent of being subjected to CDI, or combined drug intoxication."

"To what degree would his cognitive abilities be effected?"

"I believe he may have been unable to understand his actions or its consequences, due to the combination of medications prescribed for him during that time, and the behaviors associated with Klinefelter syndrome."

The prosecutor quickly stands.

"Your Honor, I object. A pharmacist is not qualified to make that statement, and her testimony is also bordering on exculpatory evidence, in that she seems to be implying the defendant didn't know he committed a crime."

She looks at Bedloe.

"Further, as defense counsel already knows, the state of Minnesota does not recognize *diminished capacity or responsibility* as a defense."

The prosecutor then turns back to the judge.

"The prosecution requests that the statement made by the witness be stricken from the record, and the jury instructed to disregard it."

Bedloe responds.

"The witness was presenting her professional opinion, one that she is immensely well qualified to make."

Guttormsen thinks for a moment, then rules.

"Objection sustained. The court reporter will strike the last response made by the witness, and the jury will disregard it."

Bedloe is thinking of giving Arneson the opportunity to expand on her many credentials, including research positions and faculty appointments, but instead, he immediately dismisses the court's absurdly biased ruling and moves on, not wanting to disrupt testimony the witness is about to present.

"Mrs. Arneson, let's examine the medications prescribed to the defendant in 2009. First of all, Vyvanse. Please provide the jury with a brief professional overview of this drug."

"Vyvanse is an amphetamine. It is a stimulant, and is indicated for the treatment of attention deficit hyperactivity disorder, also known as ADHD. Vyvanse is also sold as a street drug, is highly addictive, and has great potential for abuse."

"What is the average or normal dosage of Vyvanse for an adult with ADHD?"

"Thirty milligrams – once daily."

"And if the adult is prescribed seventy milligrams daily?"

"Well, seventy milligrams is the maximum dosage. It's powerful stuff, and like I said before, it's very addictive. Any patient would have to be in pretty bad condition for a doctor to prescribe that much on a daily basis."

"What about serious side-effects?"

"There are many possible serious side-effects with Vyvanse, especially considering the maximum dosage. They could include paranoia, delusions, visual and auditory hallucinations, just to name a few."

"If someone has been diagnosed with depression, could you understand a doctor prescribing this drug?"

"Yes, I could. Vyvanse is also indicated for the treatment of severe depression. Mr. Swain was given this medication for both that and ADHD. However, he was also taking ten milligrams of Ambien for sleep apnea. As a pharmacist, I would not fill that prescription because one of the major side-effects is *depression*. It would only increase its severity. Therefore, I would automatically have the patient ask the doctor to call me."

"All right. Now, Ambien. A brief overview, please."

"The drug is a short-acting non-benzodiazepine hypnotic medication usually prescribed for insomnia, some brain disorders, or, as in the case concerning Mr. Swain, to induce sleep in apnea patients."

The court reporter asks for a spelling of "benzodiazepine," and the witness obliges. Bedloe then asks,

"What is an average dosage for an adult?"

"Usually around five to ten milligrams, once daily. As I mentioned, Mr. Swain has sleep apnea, so the medication is usually taken just before bedtime."

"You stated that Ambien is a *hypnotic* medication. What is meant by that?"

"To my knowledge, no one quite knows, but there exists continuing evidence that a person taking Ambien appears to be hypnotized while the medication is in effect. In other words, they can actually be in a state of sleep but can still perform tasks as normally as if they were awake. That is why the patient is told to take it just before bed."

"If taken before that time, can you relate some examples of behaviors that have occurred while in this Ambien-induced sleep state?"

"Yes, but keep in mind, these are cases appearing only in some persons. They could include sleep walking, driving an automobile, binge eating, and on rare occasions, a person taking Ambien has been known to engage in *sexual parasomnia,* which is fondling or having sexual intercourse that would be rape or assault if the person were conscious."

The prosecutor springs to her feet.

*"Please. Sexual parasomnia?* How long do we have to sit here and listen to gibberish like that from this woman?"

Bedloe swiftly goes to Reese-Hall and looks ferociously at her. The prosecutor appears frightened. He continues the stare while pointing directly at Pamela Arneson. His voice is thunderously loud.

*"This woman*, Madam Prosecutor, is a pharmacist who has been employed by a prestigious medical institution for almost two decades. She is the holder of a post-master's degree in pharmaceutical science from an equally prestigious educational institution!"

While the scolding of the prosecutor continues, Judge Guttormsen stands, bangs her gavel hard and shouts, "Mr. Bedloe," several times, to no avail. Bedloe continues berating the prosecutor.

"And you have the unmitigated impudence to refer to her professional opinion as *gibberish?* How dare you, ma'am! How dare you!"

The judge responds almost as angrily.

"Counsel, you will control yourself or be removed!*"*

He replies. "I will not permit anyone to insult one of my witnesses. They will be treated with absolute respect."

The judge sits hard into her chair.

"This court is in recess for one-half hour. After which time, both the defense and prosecuting attorneys will return and conduct themselves in a professional manner for the remainder of this trial. And, if either of you does not, the offender will be held in contempt and fined ten thousand dollars or spend one year in jail. Or both. And, it will be enforced. Do you understand?"

Both say they understand. Judge Guttormsen walks out very rapidly, deeply disturbed by the atmosphere in her courtroom.

As Russell Swain is led out, Bedloe walks to Pamela Arneson.

"I'm sorry about that."

She smiles and shrugs her shoulders.

"No problem. Incidentally, is what I'm reading and listening to in the news, and hearing today, normal, everyday behavior in Minnesota courtrooms?"

Bedloe laughs.

"It has a lot to do with the Scandinavian coffee we drink. I hear a ball-bearing can float in the stuff."

*The trial resumes. Judge Guttormsen is seated, Russell Swain comes back, and Pamela Arneson walks to the witness stand.*

"The witness is still under oath. Mr. Bedloe, resume your examination."

"Mrs. Arneson, I have one more question concerning Ambien. What are the serious side-effects commonly associated with this drug?"'

"Generally, it does seem to induce more serious side-effects than Vyvanse. Both have been known to produce paranoia, delusions, and hallucinations in some patients. And, as mentioned earlier, depression. Also, other effects of this medication are ones often associated with alcohol intoxication; such as, decreased inhibitions, aggressiveness, and extroversion that seems out of character."

Bedloe then moves to the heart of this exchange.

"According to the records and reports from the MidState Medical Center, the prescription for Ambien was given to Mr. Swain on October the fifteenth, 2009, and the prescription for the maximum dose of Vyvanse the following day, the sixteenth. Is there any significance to that?"

Arneson stares wide-eyed at Bedloe, appearing bewildered. She then looks at Russell Swain.

"The next day? Within twenty-four hours? I must admit … I didn't notice that in my review of the records and reports. If that's true, considering the other drugs and what I stated earlier about the combination of Ambien and Vyvanse, it could possibly border … on being criminal."

Russell Swain puts his head down on the table and covers his face with his hands. The room is as quiet as a tomb.

The prosecutor, seeing what emotional affect the witness's statement has had throughout the courtroom, stands to object.

"Your Honor, the witness is not qualified to state whether something is or is not criminal in this court and this case."

Arneson smiles confidently at the prosecutor's evaluation of her credentials. Bedloe turns to address the bench.

"The witness was again stating her professional opinion. Being such a noted specialist in the distribution of prescribed medications, she has obviously been associated with their legal and illegal use, and can differentiate between the two. Criminality is certainly recognizable to her."

Begrudgingly, Judge Guttormsen knows what her decision must be. "The objection is overruled."

Bedloe bows theatrically to the judge, acknowledging a long awaited favorable ruling. He then returns to the witness.

The defendant is now sitting upright.

"Next, Mrs. Arneson, an anabolic steroid. Seeing your son was an adolescent when he died, and nearing young adulthood, was he involved in an androgen replacement therapy program?"

"Yes, he was."

"So, you understand the importance of this program, on both a professional level and parental one as well."

"That is correct."

"Perhaps you know that John Morehouse testified in this courtroom concerning the necessity for proper testosterone levels as it pertains to mood and behavior."

"Yes. He's widely respected, and really knows his stuff. A great man."

Prosecutor Reese-Hall mildly objects while remaining seated.

"The witness's response is opinionated, having no bearing on this case."

"Objection sustained. The witness will confine her answers to the questions asked. Continue, Mr. Bedloe."

"Mrs. Arneson, Russell Swain was being treated with testosterone prior to and during the sexual assault. Is there a usual recommended dosage?"

"Yes, one hundred to two hundred milligrams bi-monthly, depending on the person and the method."

"Are you knowledgeable concerning the side-effects associated with the injection of testosterone, or an anabolic steroid?"

"I am aware of some side-effects. There have been reported cases of what's called *'roid rage*, whereby an adolescent or adult male becomes overly aggressive and violent. Also, an anabolic steroid can create the onset of -- sleeping disorders."

"You hesitated for a moment. Why?"

"That should've been picked up as well. The doctor that diagnosed the apnea should've seen that Mr. Swain was on testosterone injections at the time."

Bedloe dramatically looks to the jury.

"What other possible side-effects are there concerning the injection of an anabolic steroid?"

The witness responds, however, she seems to be dwelling on her previous point.

"Pathological anxiety, paranoia, hallucinations, and delusions, among others."

Bedloe returns to Arneson and moves in closer to her.

"The next question is *vitally* important to this case, so take as much time as you need before responding.

"We have examined three medications; Vyvanse, Ambien, and an anabolic steroid. I asked you to list some of the side-effects for each. All three medications share many of the same ones, do they not?"

"Yes. And, the likelihood of side-effects must be multiplied by three as well, possibly four."

"Why do you say that?"

"Well, along with the 200 milligrams of testosterone and seventy milligrams of Vyvanse, I understand Mr. Swain took an overdose of four five-milligram diazepam tablets – or twenty milligrams, and ten milligrams of Ambien. As I mentioned earlier, diazepam is a benzodiazepine, and Ambien is a non-benzodiazepine. However, they share similar properties and effects."

Bedloe goes to Michael Swain, who has been writing on a legal pad, noting all the key points Arneson has made. He reaches over the rail to retrieve it, then faces the jury.

"Ladies and gentlemen, the defense will now present an analysis of what the defendant's physiological and psychological condition was on January 2, 2010, the day of the sexual assault."

He continues, using the fingers and thumb of his open hand to count off the number of factors and likely outcomes.

"Due to the multiple medications being ingested at that time, and in view of the testimony presented by earlier witnesses, Mr. Swain may very well have been experiencing *delusions, hallucinations, paranoia, pathological anxiety, and a double or triple dose of depression.*"

He puts the legal pad down on the table in order to use the fingers and thumb of his other hand to continue the count while still displaying the first five.

"Add to these, behaviors associated with alcohol intoxication; namely, *decreased inhibitions, aggressiveness, and out-of-character extroversion.* Lastly, the serious psychological disorders often found in 47, XXY males, including *impulse control and executive functioning disorders.*" He then holds both hands up above his head for all the jury to see.

"At least ten serious consequences were certainly present in my client on that fateful day. And, if I had a third hand, more could be added.

"Ladies and gentlemen of the jury, I ask you now to remember earlier testimony by Dr. Paul Lagerfeldt, who stated that during interviews with Russell Swain shortly after his arrest, he noted that Mr. Swain appeared to have developed a 'drug dependency of some kind.'

"Also, he had symptoms of schizoaffective and bipolar affective disorders, both of which Dr. Lagerfeldt agreed can create hallucinations and delusions."

Pamela Arneson nods, responding firmly:

"Mr. Bedloe, this is why I determined that what happened to this man was unpreventable, considering the circumstances."

The prosecutor shakes her head and again objects while remaining seated.

"I would remind the court and the jury, who the *victim* is in this case, and why."

Bedloe looks at Reese-Hall, responding directly to her.

"Ma'am, there were *two* victims in this case."

Bedloe tosses his glasses back on the table and returns to the witness.


"Let's talk about one of the victims, Mr. Swain's daughter. You have mentioned and are, of course, familiar with the medication *diazepam*?"

"Yes. It's a sedative, also referred to as Valium."

"It's been stated that a child over the age of six months can be given diazepam. Is that correct?"

"Basically, yes. Children of that age can use it in small amounts, and the dosage can be increased as they get older, if necessary."

"What is the average dosage prescribed to a child six months of age?"

"Oh, anywhere from three to ten milligrams daily, divided into several portions, and carefully monitored."

"What physical reaction would occur if an average twelve-year old female, such as Mr. Swain's daughter, were to take one-five-milligram diazepam?"

"If she's of normal height and weight, and in excellent health, it would make her woozy and create slightly slurred speech.  It would also mildly sedate her."

"Would it create any serious danger to her health, or perhaps cause death as a result?"

"No, not from only one-five-milligram dose.  No."

"Would it incapacitate the girl to a point of her being unaware of her surroundings, in other words, sedate her to the point of being unable to make conscious decisions?"

Pamela Arneson understands the serious nature of Bedloe's question.

"Not any more or less than giving a person of that age a small glass of wine, as is done in many cultures in other areas of the world."


Bedloe then turns and again walks to face Michael Swain. He smiles, clearly aware of this father's efforts to find the truth for his son.

After a moment, he returns to the witness.

"Mrs. Arneson, you are aware of the term, *date-rape drug?*"

"Yes, to some degree."

"Could you name them, or some of them?"

She is immediately uncertain as to why the defense attorney is introducing this subject, which appears counter-productive. The witness, however, proceeds to answer.

"Of all the drugs, alcohol is, by far, the most common.

"Then, there is gamma-hydroxybutyrate, also referred to as GHB."

Again, the court reporter asks for a spelling. Arneson obliges, but she needs a couple of attempts to get it right. Bedloe then continues, slightly irked by another interruption.

"As you previously determined, diazepam is a benzodiazepine and Ambien is a non-benzodiazepine, but they share similar properties."

The witness nods. "Yes."

Bedloe grasps the witness stand railing.

"Ma'am, as you know, GHB is also a benzodiazepine, so would Ambien and diazepam share some of the same pharmaceutical properties and effects of GHB, and it's commonly associated tranquilizing date-rape drug, *Rohypnol?*"

Anticipating an interruption, *he* spells "Rohypnol" for the court reporter. The pharmacist simultaneously smiles at counsel's knowledge, then responds after the spelling.

"Yes."

He goes to the jury, still addressing the witness. "Would another date-rape drug be what is called, a *Z-drug?*"

"Yes. Another would be the Z-drug."

He turns back to her.

"Mrs. Arneson, what is meant by the letter, 'Z'?"

She now knows where Bedloe is going, and looks down in an effort to not smile again. The subject is too serious.

"The letter 'Z' stands for *zolpidem*."

"And what is another name for zolpidem?"

The witness sympathetically looks up and at Russell Swain.

"Ambien."

Bedloe turns to face the jury, still addressing the witness.


"So, in a deplorably twisted sense of irony, on the day this now imprisoned 47, XXY adult man sexually assaulted his own daughter, he was not only taking 200 milligrams of an anabolic steroid, *and* a maximum dosage of an amphetamine, but *also* the maximum dosage of what is essentially a date-rape drug?

"All prescribed simultaneously by the MidState Medical Center!"

Reese-Hall jumps to her feet, but the witness aggressively responds before prosecution has the chance to confront Bedloe.

"*Yes.*"

The prosecutor immediately realizes there is nothing sufficient enough to sustain an objection and sits back down.

Bedloe nods and smiles to the witness.

"Thank you, Mrs. Arneson." He looks at Judge Guttormsen. "I have no more questions."

The judge looks nervously at the prosecutor.

"All right, cross-examine this witness."

Reese-Hall sits motionless for a moment. Then, she slowly lifts herself from the chair. A sense of uncertainty has crept into her attitude, but she knows she must proceed.

"Mrs. Arneson, there are two important areas I wish to explore. The first one is frequency rate for each of the medications' side-effects that you and defense counsel listed.

"Let's start with Vyvanse. Do you happen to know the percentage of frequency of side-effects people might experience taking this medication?"

"Ma'am, I can save the court a lot of time by responding generically as it applies to the side-effects and their percentage of frequency in the three medications. The fourth, diazepam, has very few side-effects if taken as directed, and not in conjunction with Ambien."

"Very well, go ahead."

The witness responds.

"The incidences of disorders such as paranoia, hallucinations, delusions, anxiety, and depression, falls anywhere from five percent to fifteen percent in all three medications, with a median of ten percent. Keep in mind that, in my professional opinion, any percentage must be multiplied by three in this case."

"I will, thank you. So, simple mathematics would therefore conclude that the probability of the defendant being adversely affected by these medications' side-effects, would fall anywhere between fifteen and forty-five percent, correct?"

"Yes."

"And, the median percentage would then be around thirty, or less than one-in-three chance the medications were responsible for serious side-effects. And more than two-thirds they weren't."

Arneson adds: "As Mr. Bedloe stated, there were other …"

"Excuse the interruption, please answer *my* question, not his statement."

"If you're only going to use …"

"Answer the question, please."

Bedloe stands.

"Objection. The prosecutor is not allowing Mrs. Arneson to answer in a fully explainable professional manner."

"Objection overruled. The witness will answer with a 'yes' or 'no.'"

"Within those parameters, I would have to answer 'yes.'"

"Thank you. The next area we'll delve into here, is the probability that Mr. Swain wasn't even taking the medications in question. How do we know he was? Granted, he was prescribed the medications, but what if he never had the prescriptions filled? Or he stopped taking them long before the rape occurred?"

She walks confidently to the jury.

"One thing we've not taken into consideration here, is the possibility that the medications had nothing to do with the criminal behavior." She returns to Arneson.

"Can you respond to that?"

"Yes, I can. Simply contact his pharmacy to see if the prescriptions were filled and picked up. Also, in reading the doctors' reports, they didn't include the patient reporting side-effects, but they did strongly indicate that Mr. Swain's state of mind, and behaviors associated with each medication's purpose, greatly improved shortly after the prescriptions were written. Or, in the case of the testosterone, given injections."

The prosecutor walks closer to the witness, smiling.

"You've heard of the *placebo effect,* have you not?"

Arneson looks at the prosecutor in amazement, and responds with a smile while simultaneously nodding in a mock serious manner.

"Yes, I have. However, it needs to be determined whether or not Mr. Swain would fall into the experimental group or the control group, and which received the inert substance in a blind or double-blind experiment."

Bedloe leans back and puts his joined hands behind his head and thinks to himself as the interaction continues, how ignorant the prosecutor's question was, and how fortunate that Michael Swain selected these defense witnesses. He turns to look at him and nods.

Reese-Hall nervously responds, not knowing what the witness is referring to.

"That's all very interesting, but doesn't substantiate that the defendant was directly affected to the extent he would rape his own daughter. If the medications improved his state of mind, please tell me what caused him to do what he did."

"Ma'am, there are positive and negative effects with each medication. Patients have to be closely monitored. Mr. Swain definitely was not. As I tried to explain to you earlier, the complex combination of medications, especially Ambien, along with his Klinefelter syndrome, created a bomb waiting to explode."

The prosecutor vigorously shakes her head.

"It's all conjecture. I have no further questions."

Bedloe smiles to the witness.

"I wish to thank Mrs. Arneson for appearing."

She acknowledges the thank you, then stands to leave, but looks uneasy for some reason.

Bedloe tells the judge:

"Your Honor, I have just one more witness in this case."

Suddenly, Arneson speaks to him. "Mr. Bedloe." He glances back.

"Before I go, could I please ask a question?"

He looks to Judge Guttormsen. "Redirect, your Honor."

The judge nods reluctantly, for there is no other legal alternative. Bedloe asks the witness to proceed, so she sits back down.

"Something has been troubling me particularly concerning the medication Mr. Swain gave to his daughter. I'm not a lawyer, but, in my professional opinion, it's a question that needs to be answered in this trial."

The attorney looks puzzled. "What is it?"

"Prior to his arrest, Mr. Swain had in his possession *six* doctor-prescribed medications, most of which are powerful and capable enough of producing *serious* mind-altering consequences.

"If he wanted to incapacitate her, and considering his own state of mind at the time, why did he use the least powerful of them all – a relatively small dose of a mild sedative?"

Bedloe and Arneson are locked in direct eye contact. The jurors stare straight ahead. Others in the courtroom are still, some look at one another and nod. The prosecutor does not respond, but Bedloe acknowledges the witness's insight.

"I agree. Why did he? The answer seems obvious.

"Thank you, ma'am. Have a safe trip home."

She is not thanked by the judge.  The defense calls its last witness.

"I now call Dr. Walter Gary."

The bailiff asks him to enter the courtroom.

*The witness is an impeccably dressed and rotund older African-American.*

*His head is completely shaved, possibly to disguise a deeply receding hairline.  He is also sporting a carefully tended gray and black handlebar mustache.*

*Dr. Gary's speaking voice is convincingly resonant and deep.*

He is sworn in, and Bedloe begins.

"Doctor, please state your occupation and place of employment."

"I am a retired psychiatrist, and was a member of the staff at the Lincoln Regional Medical Center in Lincoln, Nebraska for twenty-seven years.  I was also on the faculty at the University of Nebraska for seventeen years, teaching a course on human sexual behavior."

"Do you still reside in Lincoln?"

"Yes."

"Like the previous defense witness, you were not subpoenaed to appear at this trial. How is it that you decided to come and assist in the defense of Russell Swain?"

"I am a volunteer consultant for the National Association of Klinefelter Syndrome, and was made aware of this case by the communications director at N.A.K.S."

Bedloe says, "It is my understanding that the communications director sent you a copy of a report prepared by Michael Swain, the defendant's father, and it contains the information we are now concerned with in this trial, namely, Klinefelter syndrome and the medications prescribed for Russell Swain. Did you receive and have you thoroughly examined this report?"

"Yes, I received and examined the report."

"Dr. Gary, in your opinion as a psychiatrist, were the medications prescribed to Mr. Swain in any way responsible for his committing a sexual assault on his daughter?"

"That's almost impossible to say, at this point in time. Probable? Yes. But not just the medications, but the combination of that and Mr. Swain being an adult with KS – Klinefelter syndrome."

"Go on."

"Well, to start with a KS brain treated with two hundred milligrams of testosterone, and then throw in a drug cocktail like what was prescribed, is somewhere between heroically stupid to negligently culpable. *Heroic* because of how awful the psychological problems KS patients have, and the situations they find themselves in, like this case, so docs feel that they need to do something as part of their mandate. Therefore, they often medicate."

He looks directly at the jury.

"The difficulty I see is attributing these obvious over-medications and questionable combinations of medications with any specificity to the sexual molestation. Did it impact on normal decision-making, inhibitory behavior, aberrant thoughts, and so on? Almost certainly yes, but how do you pin specific action on it?"

Bedloe presses him on the point while Dr. Gary twists and strokes one end of his mustache.

"Could a *court* determine if the combination of Klinefelter syndrome and one or several of the medications were or were not responsible for Mr. Swain's behavior?"

The doctor glances at Bedloe while the question is being asked, and then automatically returns his gaze to the jury, letting go of the mustache.

"In my experience, there is zero chance to totally getting any court to acknowledge this at all, but having a currently licensed psychiatrist testify to the essence of the medications' side-effects might clearly help mitigate the consequences. However, it's the old *genetics versus the law* debate."

He smiles, then goes on.

"And, of course, there is also the problem that psychiatrists are as clueless about KS as the rest of the world, so other than a generic statement that basically, in a more professional way, states what I said before, and I'll say it again. 'What the medical staff at the clinic did to this man was somewhere between heroically stupid to negligently culpable.'"

Bedloe walks closer to Dr. Gary with a profoundly serious expression on his face, as he is about to take the biggest risk in the trial, if not his professional career.

"There is one more area we need to cover, doctor.

"The defendant in this case has stated that, while he assaulted his daughter, two *demons* were present in the room in the form of shadows and voices whispering to him, persuading him that what he was doing was good and acceptable."

The sound of laughter is heard in the courtroom. Prosecutor Reese-Hall turns away and places her arm over the back of the chair. She sighs loudly, saying to Bedloe:

"Counsel, is there no end to this? *Demons?*"

Bedloe ignores the prosecutor. The witness shows no facial expression. Defense continues.

"During the last half of 2009, six months prior to the assault, Mr. Swain started to report he was witnessing these phenomenal events."

Bedloe goes to the jury, some of whom are smiling.

"He told this to his wife, two ministers, a lawyer, a psychologist, and after his arrest, he told the jail pastor. At a minimum, five people were told of this before the assault occurred, and one shortly after his arrest."

He goes to his table, picks up a piece of paper, and puts on his glasses.

"Further, Ms. Lisa Larsen, an Isanti County investigator, and an earlier witness for the prosecution, stated in her report shortly after Russell Swain was arrested, and I quote:

*'I asked the defendant if his daughter MAS came to visit over New Years. The defendant stated that he did not recall what they did over Christmas break, but later remembered they flew to Houston, Texas. The defendant said that they spent New Year's Eve in Texas and believes they returned to his home on Saturday, January 2, 2010.'"*

The psychiatrist nods his head, and an agreeable smile is clearly visible. Bedloe looks back and notices Dr. Gary wants to earnestly give his assessment. However, defense counsel has a few more points to make, so he motions to the doctor to wait before he answers. He then places the report and glasses back on the table, and continues speaking to the jury.

"Within days after his arrest, Mr. Swain was informed by the jail nurse that, by order of a county psychiatrist, all of his medications were to be terminated.

"Shortly after that decision, he inevitably began to suffer severe withdrawal symptoms which continued through his confessions, interviews, and ultimately, his guilty plea."

He walks to face Russell Swain.

"While in jail during this time, he surrendered to the agony he was suffering, and gave himself up to God and the Holy Spirit."

He then goes to Michael Swain and stops.

"In the meantime, his father, who has power of attorney over all of Russell's affairs, dedicated virtually all of his time, to find the reasons why his son committed the sexual assault on his granddaughter.  He found the paramount reason in the records of the MidState Medical Center, and told his son."

Bedloe walks back to Dr. Gary.

"Upon being sent to prison, my client has been denied the psychiatric services provided by the Minnesota Department of Corrections, because he now refuses medication of any kind.

"When asked about the presence of shadows and voices since being sent to jail and then prison, Russell Howard Swain recently stated, and I quote:


*'When the Holy Spirit entered my life, protecting and guiding me, the demons left.'"*


Bedloe places his hands on the railing surrounding the witness box.  The jury members' smiles have vanished.

"Doctor.  Are you ready to give the court your professional opinion?"

"Certainly.  But I must say, you've covered the obvious quite eloquently, and have come to the only rational conclusion.  Mr. Swain *was* indeed seeing and hearing demons.

"They were visual and vocal hallucinations due to the drugs he was subjected to."

He continues.  "I should also mention, in 2004, the Department of Psychiatry at New York University found that, among the eleven adult men with Klinefelter syndrome who were tested and interviewed, ten had forms of psychiatric disturbances, and four of those ten reported hallucinations.

"Along with having KS, the four men reporting hallucinations, were on one or more of the medications similar to what was prescribed for Mr. Swain."

Bedloe smiles.  "Thank you for appearing, Dr. Gary."

He addresses the court.  "I have no further questions."

The judge responds.  "Madam Prosecutor, cross examine?"

She shakes her head.  Guttormsen coldly addresses the psychiatrist without looking at him.

"The witness is free to go."

Jeremiah Bedloe speaks.  "Your Honor, the defense rests."

"Very well. The court is therefore adjourned until tomorrow morning at nine o'clock, at which time final summations will be presented."

"All rise."

Bedloe and Michael Swain leave the courthouse, and are immediately surrounded by the press and media, mostly from Minneapolis-St. Paul, but some national correspondents as well. Amid the continuing demonstrations by protesters, the defense attorney is bombarded with questions, but wants no part of it.

He looks around the immediate area and sees Lorna and Victor walking to the parking lot, so he calls their names and they stop. He goes to them, and notices his secretary looks wonderfully healthy, and has a radiant sense of beauty. He smiles excitedly, having not seen her for five months, and asks:

"How are ya, darlin'? You-look-*terrific!*"

Lorna is wearing eye-liner and natural-based lipstick, along with a slight tint of facial makeup. Her hair is shoulder length and loosely curled. She has lost considerable weight and is wearing a fashionable dress hemmed just above the knee.

"I'm fine, JB. You?"

"Tired, but okay. Victor."

They shake hands. Lorna leans in closer to her boss. The fragrance of her perfume is evident.

"Thank you for the seats."

She then puts a hand gently on his shoulder.

"For heaven's sake, JB, I'm glad it's almost done. You look terribly beat. The spring chicken flew the coop years ago, don't you know."

Bedloe gives her a kiss on the cheek and responds warmly, "I know, I know.  Just like old times, right?"

The defense attorney and his secretary exchange a warm embrace.  He then asks:

"You two going be here tomorrow?  In court?"

Lorna nods with an emotionally sincere, sisterly smile.

"We wouldn't miss it for the world."

Tightly grasping Bedloe's hands with both of hers, his secretary continues.

"JB, whatever the outcome of this thing, you've won.  You've won."

She returns to her husband, and takes his arm.  About to leave, she concludes with:

"I will pray tonight for Russell and his daughter.

"This man does not resemble my father in any way."

# ACT THREE

## Scene One

## Closing Summations

*That same evening, the eve of closing summations.*

Janet Reese-Hall sits in the study of her family's four-bedroom ranch-style house in neighboring East Bethel, Minnesota. Her husband, Peter, a high-school assistant principal, is in the kitchen making his prize-winning chili con carne, and its pleasant spicy aroma fills the home. Their two children, Abigail, age seven, and Steven, age five, sit in the living room playing video games on the television.

She is dissecting the papers and court documents concerning the Russell Swain case, completing her summation. Sitting nearby is an empty wine glass. After reading and writing for an hour or more, she goes into the kitchen carrying the glass and says to her husband:

"Smells good."

He fills a small ladle of his chili, then blows on it before offering it to his wife. She slowly sips it, followed by the customary compliment.

"Yum. Have you ever thought about going into the chili business?"

Janet walks to the refrigerator and refills the glass with Chablis, then sits at the kitchen table. Peter makes a judgment.

"That's your third one. You've got a big day tomorrow."

She looks at the glass.

"You want it?"

"Sure. Better me than you."

Peter smiles, but knows his wife is troubled and tired.

"I can always tell, especially if there's more than one glass of wine involved, that you've 'hit the wall.' Jan, it'll soon be over."

He takes a sip of the wine. There is a significant lengthy silence.

Then Janet says, "Pete ... I'm worried."

"It's got to be the Swain case." She nods.

"I see now that the entire sentencing hearing in 2010 was saturated with omission and pre-determined conclusions. The transcript reeks of it. The victim impact statement and that woman. I have to admit, it was disgraceful. I had no idea she was telling lies."

She gets angry.

"All of this could've been avoided, if they would've just sent him to that *goddamned treatment center.*"

She swiftly turns around in her chair to see if the children heard her swear.  Peter puts the wineglass down on the table, wipes his hands on a towel and sits.  He looks at her for a minute, and then responds.

"That may be true … but he did a terrible thing."

Janet leans forward and puts her arms on the table, with hands joined.

The prosecutor tries to explain.

"If you were in the courtroom this week and listened to the defense witnesses.  Everything Bedloe and his witnesses did and said was all so darn solid and convincing.  What did I have to present in comparison?"

She kicks her legs out and slumps back in the chair with hands now joined on her lap and shakes her head, obviously in serious turmoil.

"Maybe Bedloe *was* right when he made that *estrogen* crack.

"It was so *easy* to hate Swain for what he did to his own daughter.  But now, it seems somehow equally as cruel to send him back to prison – particularly if you have conflicts within yourself, questions that are probably answerable if I wasn't biased, being a woman and having kids of my own, especially a daughter.

"I don't care much about winning or losing a case, as long as the outcome is justified, and I can look at myself in the mirror afterward.

"Cases I've prosecuted in the past, like this one, involving sex with a child and all. God, I felt like taking a long, hot soapy shower after the prosecution witnesses' testimonies were over and done with – listening to the victims and their families. It was all so cruel and ... *dirty*."

She smiles lovingly at her husband.

"You certainly knew all this, when I brought it home with me."

He nods, but remains silent.

The county prosecutor sits straight in the chair and gets up. She takes the half-full glass of wine from Peter's hand and drinks what remains, then places it on the table and bends down to give him a kiss. He feels her lower lip quivering against his.

As they search each other's eyes, Peter sees the pain on his wife's face.

Janet turns away, telling him she's going to go kiss the kids and try to get some sleep.

He says good night, and adds:

"Babe, I love you. I'm calling the school tomorrow to take off work. I'll be in the courtroom for you."

She turns back to him with eyes filled with tears, yet clearly sees the man of her dreams.

"I love you too. Don't know what I'd do without you. I'm blessed, and a lucky girl."

Again turning to leave, she takes a few steps, then stops.

"Pete ... let's go back home."

*Friday, June 15th, 2012. It is eight-forty-five a.m.*

Jeremiah Bedloe and Michael Swain arrive at the courthouse in separate vehicles. Bedloe walks to the entrance, wading through a throng of reporters and photographers, simply ignoring them.

He is carrying the two briefcases.

Once inside, Jeremiah sees Michael already seated. He goes to stand before him. Swain notices an unfamiliar expression on Bedloe's face and gets up.

The defense attorney puts the briefcases down on the floor. He grasps the handles merely by the index finger of each hand, then lifts them waist high. A big smile covers his face.

"Here you go, my friend. I do believe these heavy goddamned things I've been carrying around belong to you." Then he gets serious. "But Russell's case would've gone absolutely nowhere without them, along with a father's love for his son and granddaughter."

The father takes them and responds, "Jeremiah, thanks for everything."

Bedloe nods and glances to see Lorna and Victor already seated. He smiles and goes to his table as Russell Swain is led into the courtroom.

Michael slowly sits back down, somehow realizing that the attorney has made an important decision. What it is, he doesn't know. However, a sense of peace is clearly evident on the man's face.

"All rise."

Judge Loretta H. Guttormsen enters and sits. She scans her notes for a moment, then looks up to begin.


"Ladies and gentlemen of the jury, this case involves a first-degree felony. You are instructed to render a verdict of guilty or not guilty. If you find the defendant guilty, he will be remanded to the Minnesota Department of Corrections to complete his term of incarceration. The charges will remain the same, as will the remainder of the sentence.

"If you find the defendant not guilty, all charges will be dropped, and he will be immediately released from custody.

"There will be no plea bargaining in my court!"

Judge Guttormsen looks stone-faced at the county prosecutor.

"The prosecutor will present her closing summation."

Reese-Hall stands to address the ten jurors but momentarily remains silent, greatly disturbed by the judge's remarks.

Nevertheless, she raises her head and eyes to the ceiling. And after a deep breath to calm herself, she begins.

"I've heard it said, from law school to the courtroom that our nation's system of justice is imperfect, yet it is still the best the world has to offer. I agree. In the overwhelming majority of cases, we get it right. But occasionally, we don't.

"How does Isanti County, and the people, stack up in their judgment concerning this defendant?"

Then after another brief pause, she continues.

"Russell Howard Swain, without any reasonable doubt, has a history of sexual improprieties. He admits to them himself. The prosecution concedes that many of these improprieties were thoughts and behaviors that did not directly involve others, and perhaps some never happened.

"However, were these thoughts and behaviors directly or indirectly responsible for the deplorable event that occurred on January 2, 2010? Perhaps.

"But, really, that question is not significant.

"What is significant, is the fact that the defendant sexually assaulted his then twelve-year-old daughter. He not only confessed this behavior to his minister, but to numerous other people as well. In the process, he described what happened that day. That is why he was arrested.

"So, the question as to whether or not the incident occurred is not an issue for you to decide.

"What is on trial here is two-fold. The first issue concerns the reasons why the defendant behaved in the way he did. The second, and more important issue, is recidivism – the likelihood of his repeating this crime once freed."

She looks at Bedloe.

"In this judicial proceedings, a vital question demands an answer. Were all the reasons presented by the defense understandable and mitigating to the degree it now warrants Russell Swain's unconditional release from prison?"

Janet Reese-Hall goes to the jury and stands directly before them.

"No. They are not.

"This crime was too terrible."

She points to the defendant.

"Mr. Swain, without his daughter's knowledge, drugged her then twelve-year-old central nervous system with a mind-altering substance enough to sedate her. While the medication was mild, his motivation was for one reason, and one reason only. To have sexual intercourse with her.

"For four days we have all been subjected to the graphic details of this assault. Upon completion of these descriptions of the sexual attack, we were then told that the defendant could not control his behavior at the time.

"Which leads to the issue of all the medications prescribed for him, whose effects were compounded by his genetic disorder. Were these the reasons he could not restrain his lustful desires? Or was it due to an abiding disregard of the cruelty he imposed against a child he is said to love dearly? Was his alleged *diminished capacity,* which I remind you, is not recognized as a defense by the state of Minnesota, responsible for his behavior, or was it due to a total and complete selfish disregard for this girl?

"That, ladies and gentlemen, is what you must decide. You've heard and read all that needs to be known in order to render a verdict of unconditional freedom or a return to confinement for the duration of his sentence.

"Before your deliberation begins, please consider these very important points." She looks at Russell Swain.

"What message will be sent to thousands upon thousands of victims, and future victims, throughout this country? What message will be sent if the defendant is allowed to simply walk out of this courtroom a free man?"

Her gaze returns to the jury. "What do we say to these people? What assurances do we have that he will not commit a sex crime again? His own confessional words to a minister of God two years ago, noted his desire to attack innocent girls in the future. Does he still harbor these thoughts?

"And then, there's the alternative. Are we to believe that if sent back to prison, the defendant will be rehabilitated to the extent that, when released into society, he will not return to the behaviors that directly resulted in his arrest and incarceration?

"It's a well-publicized fact that the Minnesota Department of Corrections' sexual offender treatment program has been highly criticized for its ineptitude. However, even if it *were* effective, Mr. Swain has received no treatment, and the DOC has stated that none is anticipated for him in the foreseeable future. Why? Because he's considered a *low-level offender.*

"So, what do we have? On one hand, the defendant walks out of this courtroom a free man, with prolonged, intense therapy an option. On the other, a return to prison, where he has yet to receive any assistance. And if it is provided in the future, the quality and effectiveness will be questionable."

Judge Guttormsen looks sternly at the jury, and then furiously at Janet Reese-Hall.

The prosecutor glances momentarily at Bedloe. At first, he questions whose side she's on. But after so many years in criminal law, he quickly understands what she is trying to accomplish.

Reese-Hall concludes her summation.

"In closing, I'd like to say something personal."

Close to tears, the woman looks down and fights to remain composed, and doesn't quite succeed. Tears well in her eyes and her voice cracks.

"Like many of you, I have children of my own.

310

"On a daily basis, my husband and I live in fear knowing the world we live in. Hardly a day goes by that we don't hear of children in this country whose lives are ruined or who are injured or killed by adults they trusted, as well as strangers. There are so many victims. So many."

Reese-Hall extends her arms, appealing to the jury and everyone in the courtroom. Perhaps, with heavy media presence, she is appealing to the nation as well.

"For the love of God, how do we protect our kids? We must protect them!" She pauses for a moment, and then adds:

"This redeemable man needs specialized assistance. Now."

She slowly returns to her table, looking at Peter as she goes.

Judge Guttormsen looks coldly at the prosecutor, and then at the defense attorney.

"Counsel, your closing summation."

Bedloe remains seated, slumped in his chair. He stares at joined aged and wrinkled hands resting on his lap, thinking to himself how impressive were the emotional and courageous words from the young woman sitting at the table next to him. He looks over to her, knowing they are both weary from fighting a hidden foe.

He then gets up and walks deliberately to the front of the courtroom, to the left of the judge's bench. His hands now sit comfortably in his sport coat pockets as he stops to behold the

Statue of Justice.  He concentrates on the famous figure for a moment before beginning.

"Throughout our nation's history, sculptors and artists have replicated this time-honored symbol of American justice we see before us.  In one hand is held a sword, in the other, a scale.  The person is blindfolded."

Bedloe slowly turns and walks toward the jury box with his head down, speaking as he goes.

"What do these three symbols, so often exhibited inside and outside of courtrooms, mean to us?"

He asks the jurors to look at the statue.

"The sword symbolizes the power of reason and justice.

"The scale weighs the strengths and weaknesses of each case.

"And the blindfold?  It represents the objectivity of judge and jury, who decide the issue before the court without fear or favor.  Blind justice is impartial.

"As important as these three symbols are to our society, of *equal* importance is a fourth.  It is the one so often overlooked."

Bedloe takes his right hand out of his pocket, and points to the statue.

"The person representing our time-honored system of justice is a *young woman.*

"She is a symbol of strength and durability, of reason and fairness to all."

The same index finger now points vertically in front of him.

"One life, a beautiful girl."

The left hand leaves his pocket and also points vertically, parallel to his other hand.

"The second life, her father, who remains behind the razor-wired topped walls of punishment.

"In the eyes of so many people, even today in this very courtroom, there is no acceptable defense for sexual assault, especially involving a child.  The blindfold is to be *torn away.*"

Then he drops his hands and looks once more at the statue.

"No matter our emotions or our opinions, Lady Justice demands that the facts are to impartially determine the verdict in *every* case."

Bedloe walks to his client and stops.


"Russell Howard Swain first appeared before this court two years ago.  The county's motivation was clear from the start.  To *punish* him.  And, the punishment started even *before* he received close to the maximum prison sentence.

"Because of the nature of the crime, this particular defendant was to learn a lesson for all to witness.  He must be brought to his knees, so the public will see, that this county allows *zero tolerance* for his behavior."

The defense attorney returns to the jury.

"A transcript of that court sentencing hearing clearly documents that a stranger in town was subjected to three hours of degrading treatment. It started with an angry, vengeful local prosecutor hell bent on sending, and using her own words, *this murderer to prison for life.*

"The hearing also featured two reports submitted to the court.

"The first one was from a county employee, who upon reading my client's confessions and interviewing him, presented her conclusions. The major issue was a matter of exclusion: she did not include vital information about the defendant that would, in any way, question his guilt.

"The second report was from a state employee. She submitted her conclusions based on defense evidence, and by briefly questioning Mr. Swain. Her interpretations painted a damning portrait of my client. It showed her evaluation of him was infused with an unprofessional loathing. Why? As she later stated in this very courtroom, for the 'harm that was done to this little girl.'

"What followed soon after, was the despicable display of slander an emotionally disturbed witness was allowed to present in an American court of law. Her so-called *victim impact statement* involved ticking off the various areas of life this crime impacted on her daughter, but then veered into a completely unsubstantiated, hate-filled tirade, a self-serving character assassination leveled against her former husband. And the court, having her written statement beforehand, was therefore aware of its damaging content, and knew well that by law, it could not be challenged by the defense.

"Now, during this trial, the prosecution called the same three people as witnesses. However, unlike two years ago, their testimonies could be challenged by the defense. Once cross-examinations were completed, the trio was shown to have given written and oral testimony riddled with bias, unfounded statements, distortions, and outright lies."

Jeremiah Bedloe turns to face Janet Reese-Hall and acknowledges, yet disputes, her emotional plea to the jury.

"What message will be sent if Russell Swain is freed? It is that he has suffered enough. Enough. A one-time offender with no previous record and no other victims. A law-abiding citizen, and a non-user of alcohol or illicit drugs, whose capacity to alter his behavior was severely diminished during the year 2009."

His gaze returns to the jury.

"Let me present you with a synopsis of what happened to Russell Howard Swain during this tragic time, leading to his imprisonment.

"During the year, 2009, a year before the sexual assault on January 2, 2010, Mr. Swain's life was in turmoil because of the psychological and physical disorders he was enduring, and he sought medical help.  During that year, he was prescribed six serious medications chosen to help improve his conditions.  Within months, irrational thoughts and insane ideas started to invade his mind, culminating with hallucinations of strange malevolent shadows and voices.

"This poly pharmaceutical overdosing was prescribed on a continuing basis by the MidState Medical Center, and nowhere in court records does it show a hint of that fact until now.  One does not have to delve too far to find the reason.

"Consider this: Of the eight most addictive legally prescribed mind-altering drugs available, *four* were simultaneously medically prescribed for Mr. Swain in 2009, and were definitely in his system before and during the assault.

"Furthermore, interacting with these drugs, is the fact that my client is the involuntary recipient of a genetic chromosomal disorder, Klinefelter syndrome, that science has established, seriously alters brain functioning.  It is a life-long disability he has struggled with, and the court having been informed of this numerous times before and during the sentencing hearing, nevertheless judged it irrelevant.  In fact, the presiding judge heartbreakingly stated:


*'Klinefelter syndrome was merely an excuse by the defendant to minimize his offense.'*

"Getting back to the timeline. A week after the assault, Russell Swain emotionally confessed his sin to his minister, who, the very next morning, illegally informed the Isanti County Sheriff's Office of the confession. Within hours, my client was arrested and put into a basement jail cell.

"Soon afterward, along with devastating side-effects involved with his medications, were the inevitable torturous withdrawals he then had to endure when the county psychiatrist abruptly and suspiciously ordered the jail nurse to terminate their use. While his withdrawal symptoms were in full bloom, and without treatment for his Klinefelter syndrome, a series of irrational personal statements were made that were to seal his fate, including the guilty plea and more bizarre confessions. As a result of these, he was irredeemably judged a deviant and a threat to society by the county prosecutor's office.

"Russell Swain remained isolated in jail for eight months awaiting his sentencing hearing. This confused, honest man sobbed continuously, not understanding what had happened to him and why. And as we now know, his 'confessions' were a cry for someone to help him with answers.

"After all was said and done, what were the county and state employees' judgmental evaluations based on that led to his imprisonment? *His thoughts and words.* Nothing else was presented by the prosecution at the court sentencing hearing. The only evidence was what Mr. Swain said to his minister, and repeated while he was in jail.

"And *nowhere* does it show that *anyone* displayed a smidgeon of humanity for Mr. Swain during that entire period, nor did anyone attempt to find and examine alternative explanations for his behavior, *including*, most disturbingly, his own defense attorney at the time.

"A devastating genetic disorder and the near fatal medication cocktail, both of which this county was aware of, and deemed inconsequential.

"The callous continuing double sucker-punch leveled against this man, resulted in an unjust and unnecessarily extended prison sentence instead of probation and treatment."

Bedloe picks up the hearing transcript.

"In order to understand the court's biased attitude at that hearing concerning my client's mental and physical condition, one has only to read this document." He turns to the last paper clip while shaking his head.

"I again quote the judge.

'The offender states that, because of physical and mental impairments, he lacked substantial capacity for judgment when the offense was committed. The court finds no evidence that that factor applies here.'

"So, what does this entire religious, medical, legal, and governmental debacle leave us with today?" Bedloe throws the transcript down on the table and faces his client.

"The renowned defense witnesses have been heard in this trial, and all of them stand in agreement, that Russell Howard Swain's prognosis for the future is excellent, and they are waiting for the opportunity to give him the treatment he needs to become sound and whole.

"And, as he and his family pray, to one day soon, reunite with his daughter."

Russell emotionally erupts as his lawyer states to the jury:

"It is time for healing, not further punishment. Thank you."

He returns to his chair and concentrates on the Statue of Justice one last time, confident and content that the work he and Michael Swain have done, will yield the desired result.

Then, with a sense of realism, his mind glances back to the first day a young man entered a courtroom as a neophyte attorney just out of law school, and his baptismal trial by jury.

This trial will close his long and distinguished career.

Judge Guttormsen looks at the ten people representing the county and gives them jury instructions. She then says:

"Ladies and gentlemen, you will now retire to render a verdict in the case of the State of Minnesota v. Russell Howard Swain. This court is in recess until then."

"All rise."

## Scene Two

# The Verdict

*The next day, Saturday, six forty-five a.m.*

Jeremiah Bedloe is awakened by a ringing sound. He gains enough consciousness to fumble for the motel room telephone without sitting up.

"Who is it?"

*"Janet Reese-Hall."*

He rolls his feet to the floor and sits on the edge of the bed. Reese-Hall says,

*"It's a hung jury."*

"The hell, you say. That's what you wanted."

*"Yep. The jury was up most of the night. It was seven to three."*

"Along gender lines?"

*"I don't know. Who the hell gives a damn? Anyway, the city attorney wants both of us in the judge's office at eleven this morning."*

"I'll be there." He hangs up, and rings Swain's room.

"Michael, it's a hung jury. Let's get some breakfast."

They talk over the situation at a small diner in North Branch. Bedloe explains what is about to occur.

"A hung jury is basically a mistrial, so it's now in the lap of the Isanti County prosecutor's office and the Cambridge City Attorney. They could drop all charges, plea bargain, or order a new trial. I meet with Reese-Hall and Guttormsen this morning at eleven."

"What do you think they'll do?"

"I have no clue. But I do know one thing. Even though the judge stated there'd be no plea-bargaining, it's got to be back on the table, and they all know it."

Bedloe looks to Swain as the waitress comes out with orders of pancakes and coffee. After she leaves, he continues.

"Michael, I know your feelings about Russ' complete release, but if what I think is going to happen at the meeting does happen, it's no longer viable in their eyes. Reese-Hall's not going to drop charges unless there's an absolute assurance of mandatory therapy. Both you and I know it. So, it's either plea bargain or the whole damn thing starts over again."

Swain cuts into his thick pile of pancakes, chewing in silence while looking out the window. He takes a big swig of coffee, and suddenly pushes the plate away angrily. Bedloe hasn't even touched his yet.

"So, what's the bottom line, Jeremiah? Just sit and wait for *them* to decide? And again play their political games with my son's life?"

The defense attorney doesn't answer for a time because he's troubled. Something stinks about this whole thing. Reese-Hall knows it too. He can almost predict what the atmosphere in Guttormsen's office is going to be like, and how she'll conduct the meeting to her own advantage and that of her cronies. The thought of it pisses him off.

"No, we have some leverage. I haven't had enough time to decide the next step. After we're done here, I'm going back to my room and lie down, and think this whole damned thing through. But, my friend, I'll tell you one thing. There's going to be a major hitch to all this. I know there is."

Swain asks, "What?" Bedloe hesitates. Swain impatiently repeats himself. *"What?"*

"Guttormsen has a definite say in everything. Look, the woman doesn't give a damn about your son or your granddaughter. She'll go along with any decision as long as we agree that no civil litigation be filed against the medical center. No lawsuits."

"What about our pro bono agreement?"

Counsel digs into his pile of pancakes.

"There are ways around it. If nothing else, invite me down to Florida for a couple of weeks next winter. I want to see and hear firsthand what that 'snow-bird' bullshit is all about."

*Eleven a.m., the courthouse office of Judge Guttormsen.*

She starts the meeting.

"Let the record show that in attendance concerning the State of Minnesota v. Russell Howard Swain, are myself, Judge Loretta Guttormsen: prosecutor Janet Reese-Hall: and defense attorney Jeremiah Bedloe. The court reporter will be taking down what is said."

The judge leans back in her chair.

"So, what do we have here now?"

There is a strategic silence, as everyone jockeys for position, waiting for the other to speak first. Bedloe taps his fingertips on the table in his customary manner, and then goes for the total package, aiming high.

"Complete release. No strings attached."

Reese-Hall responds.

"No way in hell. Plea bargain with rigid stipulations."

"Stipulations? Okay, here they are. My client is to be immediately released from the Minnesota DOC, have complete freedom of mobility, and will enroll in the Alpha Human Service's outpatient treatment program."

"Outpatient? What happens then?"

"Upon successful completion at Alpha, all charges against him are to be dropped."

"And if he doesn't successfully complete the Alpha program?"

"All bets are off. It's back to Moose Lake. But, he'll complete it. He's a tad nuts right now because of everything he's gone through, however, the man is far from stupid."

Reese-Hall is in thought for a moment, then goes back to Bedloe.

"No complete release. Two years of residential in-patient at Alpha, then five years of probation. One violation of any kind, especially sexual, and it's back to the slammer."

"Not possible."

The judge strategically points the negotiations in the expected direction.

"There is also the issue of civil litigation. The court is more apt to go along with the terms once agree upon if, and only if, it includes a complete and permanent termination of this case. With prejudice. That includes all parties involved."

Both the prosecutor and the defense attorney are aware of the judge's intent. Bedloe contemplates his next move.

"Certain parties were significantly responsible for my client spending the last two years behind bars, with many more to come. As was expressed in my closing statement, he has suffered enough.

"He will agree to a 'with prejudice' stipulation, and walk out of this county penniless, only if he is completely freed and returned to the same status he held prior to his arrest.

"It will then be his personal determination what course of therapy to pursue."

Reese-Hall looks down and shakes her head.

"I'm not going to say this again. There has got to be intense therapy. There is no way in hell your client should be totally released without it. Even outpatient." She looks angrily at Bedloe.

"Sir, perhaps you do not recall *my* closing statement."

Judge Guttormsen reaches for the telephone and hits the "0" button for the receptionist. She tells her,

"Get the city attorney for me."

The room is still. Her phone rings a few moments later.

"Bert, I have Reese-Hall and Bedloe here with me. I'll put you on speaker phone.

"Done. Can you hear me?"

*"Yah. I've got a hunch you're stuck. What's going on there?"*

"Defense counsel wants a complete release with voluntary therapy. Prosecution wants to plea bargain."

*"What's the plea bargain?"*

"Two years at Alpha, then five years of stringent probation."

*"He's balking at that deal? Mr. Bedloe, it sure beats the hell out of going back to prison."*

Bedloe responds. "Complete release beats the hell out of' certain parties being sued for medical negligence, and my client receiving significant monetary damages."

*"So, what you are saying is, that you and your client will agree to no litigation – with prejudice. No future lawsuits of any kind."*

"We will consider it."

*"It's tempting, I'll say that. But jeez almighty, the media will crucify us if he walks. We can't do it. What a damn mess. Janet there, what's your thinking on this here? Do you think the prosecutor's office wants a new trial? To be honest with you, from what I've seen of the state and national media, they seem to be on our side. A new trial could end up a blessing in disguise."*

Jeremiah Bedloe is becoming increasingly irritated. Reese-Hall responds to the city attorney.

"Look, this is above my pay grade, and it's too serious a matter. But seeing you asked, my opinion is this: What's to say a new jury won't come back with the same decision – a hung jury? To me it's a waste of time and taxpayer's money. It doesn't make a bit of sense. All this because of media coverage? *Damn it, what ever happened to justice, for God's sake?"*

Bedloe stands and laughs in defiance.

"If this court orders a new trial, we're going after everybody, not just the medical center. And, my client will end up very, very wealthy. And so will his attorney. I guarantee it. So ..."

He takes hold of the manila folder he walked in with, extracts a single sheet of legal pad paper with something written on it in long hand, and slams it down on the table.

"I've heard enough. It's time for the 'players to lay down their cards.' Here's my client's final offer. Under the circumstances, it's very fair to all concerned. Accept every one of the stipulations without debate, or we sue, and then it goes on and on and on."

The defense attorney turns and abruptly walks out of the judge's office, leaving the two women sitting there, speechless.

Janet Reese-Hall calls Jeremiah Bedloe that afternoon, and requests the telephone numbers and email addresses for John Morehouse, Douglas Wilson, and Dr. Paul Lagerfeldt. She would not reveal the reason for the request, and he doesn't ask. However, Bedloe knows that his stipulations on the piece of paper are being discussed.

He gets the information requested by Reese-Hall from Michael Swain, then calls her back.

The prosecutor calls again later in the day and informs Bedloe the court will reconvene with a decision on Monday at two p.m. Other than that, he doesn't hear from the city or the county for the rest of Saturday, all day Sunday, or Monday before the decision.

*Monday, one forty-five p.m. The Isanti County Courthouse.*

The defense attorney and his client walk to their table and are met by the prosecutor, who is grinning.

"Counsel, I'll bet you're one hell of a poker player. I agree with most of the stipulations, and I must say, you 'beat the house.'"

Bedloe smiles and grasps Russell Swain's shoulder and forearm, shaking him vigorously with excitement. Swain looks at his attorney with a puzzled expression on his face. They both sit.

By court order, extra sheriff's deputies are standing by outside the courthouse with hands joined behind their backs, and more deputies are similarly posted inside.

"All rise. The Honorable Ronald D. Lynch presiding."

To the horror and fear of Russell Swain, the judge who enters the courtroom is the same one that sent him to prison in 2010. The two men have a difficult time looking at one another.

The expression on the judge's face clearly indicates he would rather be anywhere but in this courtroom. Russell leans in closer to his attorney and informs him who the man is. Bedloe nods with a devilish smile.

"I know."

Judge Lynch begins.

"Be seated.

"Due to the jury's inability to reach a unanimous verdict in this case, I must declare a mistrial prevailed. Therefore, it was the burden of the city prosecutor's office and the court, along with defense attorney's approval, to render a verdict. That has been done. While it is being read, there will be complete silence.

"Russell Howard Swain, you will stand."

Both he and his attorney do so. The judge continues.


"In the case of the State of Minnesota v. Russell Howard Swain, it is the determination of the Tenth Judicial District Court, that you be immediately released from custody."

Cheers mixed with groans of disapproval fill the room. The judge angrily bangs down with his gavel and shouts, *"Silence, or I'll clear this courtroom."*

When order is restored, he goes on. "The following stipulations are ordered in this decision.


"The first stipulation. It is the court's understanding, having been provided the necessary documentation from the executive director of the National Association of Klinefelter Syndrome, that a complete examination of you, Russell Howard Swain, be completed in order to determine needed physical and psychiatric treatment for your genetic chromosomal disorder. The court orders you to immediately and totally comply with this association's decisions as to said treatments and recommendations. All expenses will be the responsibility of you and your family.

"Seeing this treatment for Klinefelter syndrome is available only in the state of Colorado, you may travel to that location, and return immediately after its conclusion.

"The second stipulation. You are to immediately attend and thereafter successfully complete the outpatient treatment program provided by Alpha Human Services in Minneapolis. The court has been informed they await your arrival for registration. As with the first stipulation, all expenses will be the responsibility of you and your family.

"Third stipulation." The judge shakes his head slightly, clearly expressing disagreement.

"Citing noted forensic psychologist Dr. Paul Lagerfeldt's recommendation, and with proper timing, the Alpha rehabilitation program will eventually include your daughter. This will be a voluntary decision made solely by the girl involved, and it will be in the presence of a Winona County Social Services child psychologist. The joint therapy will not commence until she has reached her fifteenth birthday, which is July 23rd of next year."

Judge Lynch looks up from the list of stipulations and momentarily stares at Russell Swain.

"You sir, are to have no other contact with your daughter prior to and until the Alpha and Lagerfeldt programs are successfully completed. *None.*" He returns to the decision.

"The fourth stipulation. The court will issue a restraining order on Ms. Kathryn Trussoni, the girl's mother, stating she will cease and desist from any interference with the joint rehabilitation program concerning her daughter. Further, Ms. Trussoni will have no contact in any manner with Mr. Russell Howard Swain. If she does, it will result in her immediate arrest and incarceration, along with any financial penalties levied.

"The fifth and last stipulation. Commencing on August the first of this year, the MidState Medical Center has agreed to pay monetary damages to Russell Howard Swain in the amount of two hundred and seventy-five thousand dollars per year for the next three calendar years. The award is solely for the purpose of living expenses and treatments previously stipulated, leading to Mr. Swain's successful reintegration into society.

"These annual payments will be placed in a trust, controlled by Russell Swain's father, Mr. Michael Swain, and will be distributed as needed." The judge looks up and at Michael.

"Sir, you and your son's attorney are to meet next week with the city attorney and the medical center's legal representative to discuss the arrangements and to sign the necessary documents."

Michael nods, "Yes, Your Honor."


The judge returns to the decision.

"Mr. Russell Howard Swain, commencing tomorrow, the nineteenth of June, 2012, you are to be placed on three years of probation.  If during that period of time, you violate any provision set forth in this court's decision, or if you have committed any felony, sexual or otherwise, you will be returned to the Minnesota Department of Corrections for the remainder of your original sentence, with additional time added due to such offense.

"Further, if, by the determination of those involved in the treatment stipulations, you are derelict in your responsibilities, and through your own actions, do not successfully complete the programs set forth, you sir, will be in violation of your probation and immediately returned to the Minnesota DOC for the remainder of your sentence.

"Any probation violations will also result in the cancellation of monetary awards by the MidState Medical Center.

"Once the probation period has expired, and if there have been no violations, you will again appear before this court.  If it is determined by those individuals involved in the stipulations set forth, that all obligations have been successfully completed, you will be released from your probation and regain all rights of a United States citizen.

"Lastly, any designation as to a sexual offender will be stricken from the record."

The judge does not look at Russell Swain. "The Tenth Judicial District Court has instructed me to wish you well." He then exits the courtroom.

"All rise."


The courtroom gallery explodes with emotion, on both sides of the issue. The media quickly clamor for brief comments from everyone involved, then they leave to file their stories.

Amidst all of this, Bedloe turns and sees Lorna and Victor staring at him, smiling broadly. His secretary nods her approval.

The word "yes" forms on her lips. Then, she and her husband leave.

Russell Swain sits lifeless in the chair, unable to grasp the finality of what just occurred, and how simple it all seemed, to be in prison one day and freed the next. Bedloe sits back down, understanding his client's wish to be undisturbed for the time being. He glances quickly at him and notes that Russell is not in prayer. Then, he feels a hand on his forearm.

"Thank you, Mr. Bedloe. The Holy Spirit has answered all of my prayers. For you, my dad, and my daughter. I swear, I'll get it done. God Bless you."

The attorney puts his other hand on top of his client's and pats it affectionately.

"Son, it's time for whatever boy there is in you, to now become a man." He then looks at Russell, and referring to his chromosomal disorder, adds: "And learn to live with your 'X.'"

Russell catches the double meaning and laughs. Then, Bedloe feels hands grasping his shoulders, and turns to see Michael. He gets up and the two older men hug each other tightly.

They separate and Swain asks him, "How-in-the-hell did you pull this off?"

Bedloe takes a quick look at Russell, who remains seated, and puts his arm around Michael's shoulder. He leans in close.

"It must've come from one of those goddamned holy spirits I've been hearing so much about."

Michael looks down, smiling, and shakes his head at the sacrilegious comment.

"You're going straight to hell for that."

"I know. I've been told that before."

Then Reese-Hall walks up.

"Perhaps congratulations are inappropriate. But what the hell, congratulations. Oh, and one last thing."

She pulls him away from Swain somewhat, sporting an evil little grin, and whispers in his ear:

"If your client doesn't get the job done and recidivates, I'll personally hunt you down and fucking kill you. Then, I'll get *my* attorney to claim PMS made me do it."

Bedloe is stunned for a second, then reacts with a hearty laugh. "Madam Prosecutor, you're a grand lady."

She nods and says, "Even though my tenure in law has been brief in comparison, I must say that, you sir, are the most accomplished and honest attorney I've known. It was truly an honor."

Defense counsel bows a little, and watches as she goes to join her husband. He then scans a courtroom for the last time.

Russell has been joined by his mother and father. The three of them sit emotionally sharing the moment, and thinking of their future. It immediately enters Bedloe's mind that perhaps the most important person in the whole case, is missing – Marcianna – and he follows that thought with an agnostic's silent prayer for them all.


Jeremiah Bedloe, attorney-at-law, turns to leave. When outside on the courtroom steps, he stops to state matter-of-factly, to no one in particular:

"I foresee an excellent bottle of brandy in my not-too-distant future."

www.ingramcontent.com/pod-product-compliance
Lightning Source LLC
Chambersburg PA
CBHW060323200326
41519CB00011BA/1815